C-368 | CAREER EXAMINATION

THIS IS YOUR **PASSBOOK®** FOR ...

INSPECTOR OF MARKETS, WEIGHTS & MEASURES

NLC®

NATIONAL LEARNING CORPORATION®
passbooks.com

COPYRIGHT NOTICE

This book is SOLELY intended for, is sold ONLY to, and its use is RESTRICTED to individual, bona fide applicants or candidates who qualify by virtue of having seriously filed applications for appropriate license, certificate, professional and/or promotional advancement, higher school matriculation, scholarship, or other legitimate requirements of educational and/or governmental authorities.

This book is NOT intended for use, class instruction, tutoring, training, duplication, copying, reprinting, excerption, or adaptation, etc., by:

1) Other publishers
2) Proprietors and/or Instructors of «Coaching» and/or Preparatory Courses
3) Personnel and/or Training Divisions of commercial, industrial, and governmental organizations
4) Schools, colleges, or universities and/or their departments and staffs, including teachers and other personnel
5) Testing Agencies or Bureaus
6) Study groups which seek by the purchase of a single volume to copy and/or duplicate and/or adapt this material for use by the group as a whole without having purchased individual volumes for each of the members of the group
7) Et al.

Such persons would be in violation of appropriate Federal and State statutes.

PROVISION OF LICENSING AGREEMENTS. — Recognized educational, commercial, industrial, and governmental institutions and organizations, and others legitimately engaged in educational pursuits, including training, testing, and measurement activities, may address request for a licensing agreement to the copyright owners, who will determine whether, and under what conditions, including fees and charges, the materials in this book may be used them. In other words, a licensing facility exists for the legitimate use of the material in this book on other than an individual basis. However, it is asseverated and affirmed here that the material in this book CANNOT be used without the receipt of the express permission of such a licensing agreement from the Publishers. Inquiries re licensing should be addressed to the company, attention rights and permissions department.

All rights reserved, including the right of reproduction in whole or in part, in any form or by any means, electronic or mechanical, including photocopying, recording, or by any information storage and retrieval system, without permission in writing from the Publisher.

Copyright © 2020 by

National Learning Corporation

212 Michael Drive, Syosset, NY 11791
(516) 921-8888 • www.passbooks.com
E-mail: info@passbooks.com

PUBLISHED IN THE UNITED STATES OF AMERICA

PASSBOOK® SERIES

THE *PASSBOOK® SERIES* has been created to prepare applicants and candidates for the ultimate academic battlefield – the examination room.

At some time in our lives, each and every one of us may be required to take an examination – for validation, matriculation, admission, qualification, registration, certification, or licensure.

Based on the assumption that every applicant or candidate has met the basic formal educational standards, has taken the required number of courses, and read the necessary texts, the *PASSBOOK® SERIES* furnishes the one special preparation which may assure passing with confidence, instead of failing with insecurity. Examination questions – together with answers – are furnished as the basic vehicle for study so that the mysteries of the examination and its compounding difficulties may be eliminated or diminished by a sure method.

This book is meant to help you pass your examination provided that you qualify and are serious in your objective.

The entire field is reviewed through the huge store of content information which is succinctly presented through a provocative and challenging approach – the question-and-answer method.

A climate of success is established by furnishing the correct answers at the end of each test.

You soon learn to recognize types of questions, forms of questions, and patterns of questioning. You may even begin to anticipate expected outcomes.

You perceive that many questions are repeated or adapted so that you can gain acute insights, which may enable you to score many sure points.

You learn how to confront new questions, or types of questions, and to attack them confidently and work out the correct answers.

You note objectives and emphases, and recognize pitfalls and dangers, so that you may make positive educational adjustments.

Moreover, you are kept fully informed in relation to new concepts, methods, practices, and directions in the field.

You discover that you arre actually taking the examination all the time: you are preparing for the examination by "taking" an examination, not by reading extraneous and/or supererogatory textbooks.

In short, this PASSBOOK®, used directedly, should be an important factor in helping you to pass your test.

INSPECTOR OF MARKETS, WEIGHTS & MEASURES

DUTIES
Inspects, tests, and investigates a wide variety of commercial practices, in stores, markets, wholesale houses, gasoline stations, and other establishments to determine legal acceptability of weighing and measuring devices for commercial use, and for compliance with agriculture and markets laws, rules and regulations; performs related duties as required.

An employee in this class performs field inspection work involving responsibility for testing weighing and/or measuring equipment to determine its accuracy in compliance with prescribed standards. The inspections are intended to prevent fraud and deception on the part of owners of the equipment as well as to discover faulty mechanisms where no violations are intended. Inspections are made as part of an organized program or as a result of complaints. An employee in this class is a peace officer as designated under Criminal Procedure Law. Work is supervised by administrative supervisors and by State Inspectors by means of daily instructions, weekly activity reports and re-inspections of weighing and measuring devices. Does related work as required.

SCOPE OF THE EXAMINATION
The written test is designed to evaluate knowledge, skills and /or abilities in the following areas:
1. **Inspection and interviewing techniques** - These questions test your ability to select the proper course of action in situations which might occur during routine inspections. Question topics may cover, but will not be limited to, such areas as interviewing, gathering information and evidence, maintaining proper attitude, and handling irregularities and violations with integrity and sound judgment. Some questions may be in a situational format while others may deal with the proper principles and practices of inspection.
2. **Preparing written material** - These questions test for the ability to present information clearly and accurately, and to organize paragraphs logically and comprehensibly. For some questions, you will be given information in two or three sentences followed by four restatements of the information. You must then choose the best version. For other questions, you will be given paragraphs with their sentences out of order. You must then choose, from four suggestions, the best order for the sentences.
3. **Determining the accuracy of scales** - These questions are designed to test a candidate's ability to determine if weighing scales are reading accurately and, if not, the extent of error associated with each scale. The candidate is shown a test load and given the weights of single units in the load and must calculate the total weight of the test load. The candidate is also shown two separate scale readings and must determine if either or both readings are fast or slow and by how much. Knowledge of addition, subtraction, multiplication and division will be necessary. Specific knowledge of weights and scales is not required.
4. **Understanding and interpreting written material** - These questions test how well you comprehend written material. You will be provided with brief reading selections and will be asked questions about the selections. All the information required to answer the questions will be presented in the selections; you will not be required to have any special knowledge relating to the subject areas of the selections.
5. **Weights and measures** - These questions test candidates' knowledge of the various types of weighing and measuring devices and systems commonly used throughout business and industry. They deal with, but are not necessarily limited to, such areas as
    -The conversion of weights and measures from the Metric System to the English System and from the English System to the Metric System;
    -Types of linear and liquid measuring devices in common use;
    -Various types of weighing devices in common use;
    -Basic construction and operation of the various types of weighing and measuring in common use.

HOW TO TAKE A TEST

I. YOU MUST PASS AN EXAMINATION

A. *WHAT EVERY CANDIDATE SHOULD KNOW*

Examination applicants often ask us for help in preparing for the written test. What can I study in advance? What kinds of questions will be asked? How will the test be given? How will the papers be graded?

As an applicant for a civil service examination, you may be wondering about some of these things. Our purpose here is to suggest effective methods of advance study and to describe civil service examinations.

Your chances for success on this examination can be increased if you know how to prepare. Those "pre-examination jitters" can be reduced if you know what to expect. You can even experience an adventure in good citizenship if you know why civil service exams are given.

B. *WHY ARE CIVIL SERVICE EXAMINATIONS GIVEN?*

Civil service examinations are important to you in two ways. As a citizen, you want public jobs filled by employees who know how to do their work. As a job seeker, you want a fair chance to compete for that job on an equal footing with other candidates. The best-known means of accomplishing this two-fold goal is the competitive examination.

Exams are widely publicized throughout the nation. They may be administered for jobs in federal, state, city, municipal, town or village governments or agencies.

Any citizen may apply, with some limitations, such as the age or residence of applicants. Your experience and education may be reviewed to see whether you meet the requirements for the particular examination. When these requirements exist, they are reasonable and applied consistently to all applicants. Thus, a competitive examination may cause you some uneasiness now, but it is your privilege and safeguard.

C. *HOW ARE CIVIL SERVICE EXAMS DEVELOPED?*

Examinations are carefully written by trained technicians who are specialists in the field known as "psychological measurement," in consultation with recognized authorities in the field of work that the test will cover. These experts recommend the subject matter areas or skills to be tested; only those knowledges or skills important to your success on the job are included. The most reliable books and source materials available are used as references. Together, the experts and technicians judge the difficulty level of the questions.

Test technicians know how to phrase questions so that the problem is clearly stated. Their ethics do not permit "trick" or "catch" questions. Questions may have been tried out on sample groups, or subjected to statistical analysis, to determine their usefulness.

Written tests are often used in combination with performance tests, ratings of training and experience, and oral interviews. All of these measures combine to form the best-known means of finding the right person for the right job.

II. HOW TO PASS THE WRITTEN TEST

A. NATURE OF THE EXAMINATION

To prepare intelligently for civil service examinations, you should know how they differ from school examinations you have taken. In school you were assigned certain definite pages to read or subjects to cover. The examination questions were quite detailed and usually emphasized memory. Civil service exams, on the other hand, try to discover your present ability to perform the duties of a position, plus your potentiality to learn these duties. In other words, a civil service exam attempts to predict how successful you will be. Questions cover such a broad area that they cannot be as minute and detailed as school exam questions.

In the public service similar kinds of work, or positions, are grouped together in one "class." This process is known as *position-classification*. All the positions in a class are paid according to the salary range for that class. One class title covers all of these positions, and they are all tested by the same examination.

B. FOUR BASIC STEPS

1) Study the announcement

How, then, can you know what subjects to study? Our best answer is: "Learn as much as possible about the class of positions for which you've applied." The exam will test the knowledge, skills and abilities needed to do the work.

Your most valuable source of information about the position you want is the official exam announcement. This announcement lists the training and experience qualifications. Check these standards and apply only if you come reasonably close to meeting them.

The brief description of the position in the examination announcement offers some clues to the subjects which will be tested. Think about the job itself. Review the duties in your mind. Can you perform them, or are there some in which you are rusty? Fill in the blank spots in your preparation.

Many jurisdictions preview the written test in the exam announcement by including a section called "Knowledge and Abilities Required," "Scope of the Examination," or some similar heading. Here you will find out specifically what fields will be tested.

2) Review your own background

Once you learn in general what the position is all about, and what you need to know to do the work, ask yourself which subjects you already know fairly well and which need improvement. You may wonder whether to concentrate on improving your strong areas or on building some background in your fields of weakness. When the announcement has specified "some knowledge" or "considerable knowledge," or has used adjectives like "beginning principles of..." or "advanced ... methods," you can get a clue as to the number and difficulty of questions to be asked in any given field. More questions, and hence broader coverage, would be included for those subjects which are more important in the work. Now weigh your strengths and weaknesses against the job requirements and prepare accordingly.

3) Determine the level of the position

Another way to tell how intensively you should prepare is to understand the level of the job for which you are applying. Is it the entering level? In other words, is this the position in which beginners in a field of work are hired? Or is it an intermediate or advanced level? Sometimes this is indicated by such words as "Junior" or "Senior" in the class title. Other jurisdictions use Roman numerals to designate the level – Clerk I, Clerk II, for example. The word "Supervisor" sometimes appears in the title. If the level is not indicated by the title, check the description of duties. Will you be working under very close supervision, or will you have responsibility for independent decisions in this work?

4) Choose appropriate study materials

Now that you know the subjects to be examined and the relative amount of each subject to be covered, you can choose suitable study materials. For beginning level jobs, or even advanced ones, if you have a pronounced weakness in some aspect of your training, read a modern, standard textbook in that field. Be sure it is up to date and has general coverage. Such books are normally available at your library, and the librarian will be glad to help you locate one. For entry-level positions, questions of appropriate difficulty are chosen – neither highly advanced questions, nor those too simple. Such questions require careful thought but not advanced training.

If the position for which you are applying is technical or advanced, you will read more advanced, specialized material. If you are already familiar with the basic principles of your field, elementary textbooks would waste your time. Concentrate on advanced textbooks and technical periodicals. Think through the concepts and review difficult problems in your field.

These are all general sources. You can get more ideas on your own initiative, following these leads. For example, training manuals and publications of the government agency which employs workers in your field can be useful, particularly for technical and professional positions. A letter or visit to the government department involved may result in more specific study suggestions, and certainly will provide you with a more definite idea of the exact nature of the position you are seeking.

III. KINDS OF TESTS

Tests are used for purposes other than measuring knowledge and ability to perform specified duties. For some positions, it is equally important to test ability to make adjustments to new situations or to profit from training. In others, basic mental abilities not dependent on information are essential. Questions which test these things may not appear as pertinent to the duties of the position as those which test for knowledge and information. Yet they are often highly important parts of a fair examination. For very general questions, it is almost impossible to help you direct your study efforts. What we can do is to point out some of the more common of these general abilities needed in public service positions and describe some typical questions.

1) General information

Broad, general information has been found useful for predicting job success in some kinds of work. This is tested in a variety of ways, from vocabulary lists to questions about current events. Basic background in some field of work, such as sociology or economics, may be sampled in a group of questions. Often these are principles which have become familiar to most persons through exposure rather than through formal training. It is difficult to advise you how to study for these questions; being alert to the world around you is our best suggestion.

2) Verbal ability

An example of an ability needed in many positions is verbal or language ability. Verbal ability is, in brief, the ability to use and understand words. Vocabulary and grammar tests are typical measures of this ability. Reading comprehension or paragraph interpretation questions are common in many kinds of civil service tests. You are given a paragraph of written material and asked to find its central meaning.

3) Numerical ability

Number skills can be tested by the familiar arithmetic problem, by checking paired lists of numbers to see which are alike and which are different, or by interpreting charts and graphs. In the latter test, a graph may be printed in the test booklet which you are asked to use as the basis for answering questions.

4) Observation

A popular test for law-enforcement positions is the observation test. A picture is shown to you for several minutes, then taken away. Questions about the picture test your ability to observe both details and larger elements.

5) Following directions

In many positions in the public service, the employee must be able to carry out written instructions dependably and accurately. You may be given a chart with several columns, each column listing a variety of information. The questions require you to carry out directions involving the information given in the chart.

6) Skills and aptitudes

Performance tests effectively measure some manual skills and aptitudes. When the skill is one in which you are trained, such as typing or shorthand, you can practice. These tests are often very much like those given in business school or high school courses. For many of the other skills and aptitudes, however, no short-time preparation can be made. Skills and abilities natural to you or that you have developed throughout your lifetime are being tested.

Many of the general questions just described provide all the data needed to answer the questions and ask you to use your reasoning ability to find the answers. Your best preparation for these tests, as well as for tests of facts and ideas, is to be at your physical and mental best. You, no doubt, have your own methods of getting into an exam-taking mood and keeping "in shape." The next section lists some ideas on this subject.

IV. KINDS OF QUESTIONS

Only rarely is the "essay" question, which you answer in narrative form, used in civil service tests. Civil service tests are usually of the short-answer type. Full instructions for answering these questions will be given to you at the examination. But in case this is your first experience with short-answer questions and separate answer sheets, here is what you need to know:

1) Multiple-choice Questions

Most popular of the short-answer questions is the "multiple choice" or "best answer" question. It can be used, for example, to test for factual knowledge, ability to solve problems or judgment in meeting situations found at work.

A multiple-choice question is normally one of three types—
- It can begin with an incomplete statement followed by several possible endings. You are to find the one ending which *best* completes the statement, although some of the others may not be entirely wrong.
- It can also be a complete statement in the form of a question which is answered by choosing one of the statements listed.
- It can be in the form of a problem – again you select the best answer.

Here is an example of a multiple-choice question with a discussion which should give you some clues as to the method for choosing the right answer:

When an employee has a complaint about his assignment, the action which will *best* help him overcome his difficulty is to
- A. discuss his difficulty with his coworkers
- B. take the problem to the head of the organization
- C. take the problem to the person who gave him the assignment
- D. say nothing to anyone about his complaint

In answering this question, you should study each of the choices to find which is best. Consider choice "A" – Certainly an employee may discuss his complaint with fellow employees, but no change or improvement can result, and the complaint remains unresolved. Choice "B" is a poor choice since the head of the organization probably does not know what assignment you have been given, and taking your problem to him is known as "going over the head" of the supervisor. The supervisor, or person who made the assignment, is the person who can clarify it or correct any injustice. Choice "C" is, therefore, correct. To say nothing, as in choice "D," is unwise. Supervisors have and interest in knowing the problems employees are facing, and the employee is seeking a solution to his problem.

2) True/False Questions

The "true/false" or "right/wrong" form of question is sometimes used. Here a complete statement is given. Your job is to decide whether the statement is right or wrong.

SAMPLE: A roaming cell-phone call to a nearby city costs less than a non-roaming call to a distant city.

This statement is wrong, or false, since roaming calls are more expensive.

This is not a complete list of all possible question forms, although most of the others are variations of these common types. You will always get complete directions for answering questions. Be sure you understand *how* to mark your answers – ask questions until you do.

V. RECORDING YOUR ANSWERS

Computer terminals are used more and more today for many different kinds of exams.

For an examination with very few applicants, you may be told to record your answers in the test booklet itself. Separate answer sheets are much more common. If this separate answer sheet is to be scored by machine – and this is often the case – it is highly important that you mark your answers correctly in order to get credit.

An electronic scoring machine is often used in civil service offices because of the speed with which papers can be scored. Machine-scored answer sheets must be marked with a pencil, which will be given to you. This pencil has a high graphite content which responds to the electronic scoring machine. As a matter of fact, stray dots may register as answers, so do not let your pencil rest on the answer sheet while you are pondering the correct answer. Also, if your pencil lead breaks or is otherwise defective, ask for another.

Since the answer sheet will be dropped in a slot in the scoring machine, be careful not to bend the corners or get the paper crumpled.

The answer sheet normally has five vertical columns of numbers, with 30 numbers to a column. These numbers correspond to the question numbers in your test booklet. After each number, going across the page are four or five pairs of dotted lines. These short dotted lines have small letters or numbers above them. The first two pairs may also have a "T" or "F" above the letters. This indicates that the first two pairs only are to be used if the questions are of the true-false type. If the questions are multiple choice, disregard the "T" and "F" and pay attention only to the small letters or numbers.

Answer your questions in the manner of the sample that follows:

32. The largest city in the United States is
    A. Washington, D.C.
    B. New York City
    C. Chicago
    D. Detroit
    E. San Francisco

1) Choose the answer you think is best. (New York City is the largest, so "B" is correct.)
2) Find the row of dotted lines numbered the same as the question you are answering. (Find row number 32)
3) Find the pair of dotted lines corresponding to the answer. (Find the pair of lines under the mark "B.")
4) Make a solid black mark between the dotted lines.

VI. BEFORE THE TEST

Common sense will help you find procedures to follow to get ready for an examination. Too many of us, however, overlook these sensible measures. Indeed, nervousness and fatigue have been found to be the most serious reasons why applicants fail to do their best on civil service tests. Here is a list of reminders:

- Begin your preparation early – Don't wait until the last minute to go scurrying around for books and materials or to find out what the position is all about.
- Prepare continuously – An hour a night for a week is better than an all-night cram session. This has been definitely established. What is more, a night a week for a month will return better dividends than crowding your study into a shorter period of time.
- Locate the place of the exam – You have been sent a notice telling you when and where to report for the examination. If the location is in a different town or otherwise unfamiliar to you, it would be well to inquire the best route and learn something about the building.
- Relax the night before the test – Allow your mind to rest. Do not study at all that night. Plan some mild recreation or diversion; then go to bed early and get a good night's sleep.
- Get up early enough to make a leisurely trip to the place for the test – This way unforeseen events, traffic snarls, unfamiliar buildings, etc. will not upset you.
- Dress comfortably – A written test is not a fashion show. You will be known by number and not by name, so wear something comfortable.
- Leave excess paraphernalia at home – Shopping bags and odd bundles will get in your way. You need bring only the items mentioned in the official notice you received; usually everything you need is provided. Do not bring reference books to the exam. They will only confuse those last minutes and be taken away from you when in the test room.
- Arrive somewhat ahead of time – If because of transportation schedules you must get there very early, bring a newspaper or magazine to take your mind off yourself while waiting.
- Locate the examination room – When you have found the proper room, you will be directed to the seat or part of the room where you will sit. Sometimes you are given a sheet of instructions to read while you are waiting. Do not fill out any forms until you are told to do so; just read them and be prepared.
- Relax and prepare to listen to the instructions
- If you have any physical problem that may keep you from doing your best, be sure to tell the test administrator. If you are sick or in poor health, you really cannot do your best on the exam. You can come back and take the test some other time.

VII. AT THE TEST

The day of the test is here and you have the test booklet in your hand. The temptation to get going is very strong. Caution! There is more to success than knowing the right answers. You must know how to identify your papers and understand variations in the type of short-answer question used in this particular examination. Follow these suggestions for maximum results from your efforts:

1) Cooperate with the monitor

The test administrator has a duty to create a situation in which you can be as much at ease as possible. He will give instructions, tell you when to begin, check to see that you are marking your answer sheet correctly, and so on. He is not there to guard you, although he will see that your competitors do not take unfair advantage. He wants to help you do your best.

2) Listen to all instructions

Don't jump the gun! Wait until you understand all directions. In most civil service tests you get more time than you need to answer the questions. So don't be in a hurry. Read each word of instructions until you clearly understand the meaning. Study the examples, listen to all announcements and follow directions. Ask questions if you do not understand what to do.

3) Identify your papers

Civil service exams are usually identified by number only. You will be assigned a number; you must not put your name on your test papers. Be sure to copy your number correctly. Since more than one exam may be given, copy your exact examination title.

4) Plan your time

Unless you are told that a test is a "speed" or "rate of work" test, speed itself is usually not important. Time enough to answer all the questions will be provided, but this does not mean that you have all day. An overall time limit has been set. Divide the total time (in minutes) by the number of questions to determine the approximate time you have for each question.

5) Do not linger over difficult questions

If you come across a difficult question, mark it with a paper clip (useful to have along) and come back to it when you have been through the booklet. One caution if you do this – be sure to skip a number on your answer sheet as well. Check often to be sure that you have not lost your place and that you are marking in the row numbered the same as the question you are answering.

6) Read the questions

Be sure you know what the question asks! Many capable people are unsuccessful because they failed to *read* the questions correctly.

7) Answer all questions

Unless you have been instructed that a penalty will be deducted for incorrect answers, it is better to guess than to omit a question.

8) Speed tests

It is often better NOT to guess on speed tests. It has been found that on timed tests people are tempted to spend the last few seconds before time is called in marking answers at random – without even reading them – in the hope of picking up a few extra points. To discourage this practice, the instructions may warn you that your score will be "corrected" for guessing. That is, a penalty will be applied. The incorrect answers will be deducted from the correct ones, or some other penalty formula will be used.

9) Review your answers

If you finish before time is called, go back to the questions you guessed or omitted to give them further thought. Review other answers if you have time.

10) Return your test materials

If you are ready to leave before others have finished or time is called, take ALL your materials to the monitor and leave quietly. Never take any test material with you. The monitor can discover whose papers are not complete, and taking a test booklet may be grounds for disqualification.

VIII. EXAMINATION TECHNIQUES

1) Read the general instructions carefully. These are usually printed on the first page of the exam booklet. As a rule, these instructions refer to the timing of the examination; the fact that you should not start work until the signal and must stop work at a signal, etc. If there are any *special* instructions, such as a choice of questions to be answered, make sure that you note this instruction carefully.

2) When you are ready to start work on the examination, that is as soon as the signal has been given, read the instructions to each question booklet, underline any key words or phrases, such as *least, best, outline, describe* and the like. In this way you will tend to answer as requested rather than discover on reviewing your paper that you *listed without describing*, that you selected the *worst* choice rather than the *best* choice, etc.

3) If the examination is of the objective or multiple-choice type – that is, each question will also give a series of possible answers: A, B, C or D, and you are called upon to select the best answer and write the letter next to that answer on your answer paper – it is advisable to start answering each question in turn. There may be anywhere from 50 to 100 such questions in the three or four hours allotted and you can see how much time would be taken if you read through all the questions before beginning to answer any. Furthermore, if you come across a question or group of questions which you know would be difficult to answer, it would undoubtedly affect your handling of all the other questions.

4) If the examination is of the essay type and contains but a few questions, it is a moot point as to whether you should read all the questions before starting to answer any one. Of course, if you are given a choice – say five out of seven and the like – then it is essential to read all the questions so you can eliminate the two that are most difficult. If, however, you are asked to answer all the questions, there may be danger in trying to answer the easiest one first because you may find that you will spend too much time on it. The best technique is to answer the first question, then proceed to the second, etc.

5) Time your answers. Before the exam begins, write down the time it started, then add the time allowed for the examination and write down the time it must be completed, then divide the time available somewhat as follows:

- If 3-1/2 hours are allowed, that would be 210 minutes. If you have 80 objective-type questions, that would be an average of 2-1/2 minutes per question. Allow yourself no more than 2 minutes per question, or a total of 160 minutes, which will permit about 50 minutes to review.
- If for the time allotment of 210 minutes there are 7 essay questions to answer, that would average about 30 minutes a question. Give yourself only 25 minutes per question so that you have about 35 minutes to review.

6) The most important instruction is to *read each question* and make sure you know what is wanted. The second most important instruction is to *time yourself properly* so that you answer every question. The third most important instruction is to *answer every question*. Guess if you have to but include something for each question. Remember that you will receive no credit for a blank and will probably receive some credit if you write something in answer to an essay question. If you guess a letter – say "B" for a multiple-choice question – you may have guessed right. If you leave a blank as an answer to a multiple-choice question, the examiners may respect your feelings but it will not add a point to your score. Some exams may penalize you for wrong answers, so in such cases *only*, you may not want to guess unless you have some basis for your answer.

7) Suggestions
   a. Objective-type questions
      1. Examine the question booklet for proper sequence of pages and questions
      2. Read all instructions carefully
      3. Skip any question which seems too difficult; return to it after all other questions have been answered
      4. Apportion your time properly; do not spend too much time on any single question or group of questions
      5. Note and underline key words – *all, most, fewest, least, best, worst, same, opposite,* etc.
      6. Pay particular attention to negatives
      7. Note unusual option, e.g., unduly long, short, complex, different or similar in content to the body of the question
      8. Observe the use of "hedging" words – *probably, may, most likely,* etc.
      9. Make sure that your answer is put next to the same number as the question
      10. Do not second-guess unless you have good reason to believe the second answer is definitely more correct
      11. Cross out original answer if you decide another answer is more accurate; do not erase until you are ready to hand your paper in
      12. Answer all questions; guess unless instructed otherwise
      13. Leave time for review

   b. Essay questions
      1. Read each question carefully
      2. Determine exactly what is wanted. Underline key words or phrases.
      3. Decide on outline or paragraph answer

4. Include many different points and elements unless asked to develop any one or two points or elements
5. Show impartiality by giving pros and cons unless directed to select one side only
6. Make and write down any assumptions you find necessary to answer the questions
7. Watch your English, grammar, punctuation and choice of words
8. Time your answers; don't crowd material

8) Answering the essay question

Most essay questions can be answered by framing the specific response around several key words or ideas. Here are a few such key words or ideas:

M's: manpower, materials, methods, money, management
P's: purpose, program, policy, plan, procedure, practice, problems, pitfalls, personnel, public relations

   a. Six basic steps in handling problems:
      1. Preliminary plan and background development
      2. Collect information, data and facts
      3. Analyze and interpret information, data and facts
      4. Analyze and develop solutions as well as make recommendations
      5. Prepare report and sell recommendations
      6. Install recommendations and follow up effectiveness

   b. Pitfalls to avoid
      1. *Taking things for granted* – A statement of the situation does not necessarily imply that each of the elements is necessarily true; for example, a complaint may be invalid and biased so that all that can be taken for granted is that a complaint has been registered
      2. *Considering only one side of a situation* – Wherever possible, indicate several alternatives and then point out the reasons you selected the best one
      3. *Failing to indicate follow up* – Whenever your answer indicates action on your part, make certain that you will take proper follow-up action to see how successful your recommendations, procedures or actions turn out to be
      4. *Taking too long in answering any single question* – Remember to time your answers properly

IX. AFTER THE TEST

Scoring procedures differ in detail among civil service jurisdictions although the general principles are the same. Whether the papers are hand-scored or graded by machine we have described, they are nearly always graded by number. That is, the person who marks the paper knows only the number – never the name – of the applicant. Not until all the papers have been graded will they be matched with names. If other tests, such as training and experience or oral interview ratings have been given, scores will be combined. Different parts of the examination usually have different weights. For example, the written test might count 60 percent of the final grade, and a rating of training and experience 40 percent. In many jurisdictions, veterans will have a certain number of points added to their grades.

After the final grade has been determined, the names are placed in grade order and an eligible list is established. There are various methods for resolving ties between those who get the same final grade – probably the most common is to place first the name of the person whose application was received first. Job offers are made from the eligible list in the order the names appear on it. You will be notified of your grade and your rank as soon as all these computations have been made. This will be done as rapidly as possible.

People who are found to meet the requirements in the announcement are called "eligibles." Their names are put on a list of eligible candidates. An eligible's chances of getting a job depend on how high he stands on this list and how fast agencies are filling jobs from the list.

When a job is to be filled from a list of eligibles, the agency asks for the names of people on the list of eligibles for that job. When the civil service commission receives this request, it sends to the agency the names of the three people highest on this list. Or, if the job to be filled has specialized requirements, the office sends the agency the names of the top three persons who meet these requirements from the general list.

The appointing officer makes a choice from among the three people whose names were sent to him. If the selected person accepts the appointment, the names of the others are put back on the list to be considered for future openings.

That is the rule in hiring from all kinds of eligible lists, whether they are for typist, carpenter, chemist, or something else. For every vacancy, the appointing officer has his choice of any one of the top three eligibles on the list. This explains why the person whose name is on top of the list sometimes does not get an appointment when some of the persons lower on the list do. If the appointing officer chooses the second or third eligible, the No. 1 eligible does not get a job at once, but stays on the list until he is appointed or the list is terminated.

X. HOW TO PASS THE INTERVIEW TEST

The examination for which you applied requires an oral interview test. You have already taken the written test and you are now being called for the interview test – the final part of the formal examination.

You may think that it is not possible to prepare for an interview test and that there are no procedures to follow during an interview. Our purpose is to point out some things you can do in advance that will help you and some good rules to follow and pitfalls to avoid while you are being interviewed.

What is an interview supposed to test?

The written examination is designed to test the technical knowledge and competence of the candidate; the oral is designed to evaluate intangible qualities, not readily measured otherwise, and to establish a list showing the relative fitness of each candidate – as measured against his competitors – for the position sought. Scoring is not on the basis of "right" and "wrong," but on a sliding scale of values ranging from "not passable" to "outstanding." As a matter of fact, it is possible to achieve a relatively low score without a single "incorrect" answer because of evident weakness in the qualities being measured.

Occasionally, an examination may consist entirely of an oral test – either an individual or a group oral. In such cases, information is sought concerning the technical knowledges and abilities of the candidate, since there has been no written examination for this purpose. More commonly, however, an oral test is used to supplement a written examination.

Who conducts interviews?

The composition of oral boards varies among different jurisdictions. In nearly all, a representative of the personnel department serves as chairman. One of the members of the board may be a representative of the department in which the candidate would work. In some cases, "outside experts" are used, and, frequently, a businessman or some other representative of the general public is asked to serve. Labor and management or other special groups may be represented. The aim is to secure the services of experts in the appropriate field.

However the board is composed, it is a good idea (and not at all improper or unethical) to ascertain in advance of the interview who the members are and what groups they represent. When you are introduced to them, you will have some idea of their backgrounds and interests, and at least you will not stutter and stammer over their names.

What should be done before the interview?

While knowledge about the board members is useful and takes some of the surprise element out of the interview, there is other preparation which is more substantive. It *is* possible to prepare for an oral interview – in several ways:

1) Keep a copy of your application and review it carefully before the interview

This may be the only document before the oral board, and the starting point of the interview. Know what education and experience you have listed there, and the sequence and dates of all of it. Sometimes the board will ask you to review the highlights of your experience for them; you should not have to hem and haw doing it.

2) Study the class specification and the examination announcement

Usually, the oral board has one or both of these to guide them. The qualities, characteristics or knowledges required by the position sought are stated in these documents. They offer valuable clues as to the nature of the oral interview. For example, if the job involves supervisory responsibilities, the announcement will usually indicate that knowledge of modern supervisory methods and the qualifications of the candidate as a supervisor will be tested. If so, you can expect such questions, frequently in the form of a hypothetical situation which you are expected to solve. NEVER go into an oral without knowledge of the duties and responsibilities of the job you seek.

3) Think through each qualification required

Try to visualize the kind of questions you would ask if you were a board member. How well could you answer them? Try especially to appraise your own knowledge and background in each area, *measured against the job sought*, and identify any areas in which you are weak. Be critical and realistic – do not flatter yourself.

4) Do some general reading in areas in which you feel you may be weak

For example, if the job involves supervision and your past experience has NOT, some general reading in supervisory methods and practices, particularly in the field of human relations, might be useful. Do NOT study agency procedures or detailed manuals. The oral board will be testing your understanding and capacity, not your memory.

5) Get a good night's sleep and watch your general health and mental attitude

You will want a clear head at the interview. Take care of a cold or any other minor ailment, and of course, no hangovers.

What should be done on the day of the interview?

Now comes the day of the interview itself. Give yourself plenty of time to get there. Plan to arrive somewhat ahead of the scheduled time, particularly if your appointment is in the fore part of the day. If a previous candidate fails to appear, the board might be ready for you a bit early. By early afternoon an oral board is almost invariably behind schedule if there are many candidates, and you may have to wait. Take along a book or magazine to read, or your application to review, but leave any extraneous material in the waiting room when you go in for your interview. In any event, relax and compose yourself.

The matter of dress is important. The board is forming impressions about you – from your experience, your manners, your attitude, and your appearance. Give your personal appearance careful attention. Dress your best, but not your flashiest. Choose conservative, appropriate clothing, and be sure it is immaculate. This is a business interview, and your appearance should indicate that you regard it as such. Besides, being well groomed and properly dressed will help boost your confidence.

Sooner or later, someone will call your name and escort you into the interview room. *This is it.* From here on you are on your own. It is too late for any more preparation. But remember, you asked for this opportunity to prove your fitness, and you are here because your request was granted.

What happens when you go in?

The usual sequence of events will be as follows: The clerk (who is often the board stenographer) will introduce you to the chairman of the oral board, who will introduce you to the other members of the board. Acknowledge the introductions before you sit down. Do not be surprised if you find a microphone facing you or a stenotypist sitting by. Oral interviews are usually recorded in the event of an appeal or other review.

Usually the chairman of the board will open the interview by reviewing the highlights of your education and work experience from your application – primarily for the benefit of the other members of the board, as well as to get the material into the record. Do not interrupt or comment unless there is an error or significant misinterpretation; if that is the case, do not hesitate. But do not quibble about insignificant matters. Also, he will usually ask you some question about your education, experience or your present job – partly to get you to start talking and to establish the interviewing "rapport." He may start the actual questioning, or turn it over to one of the other members. Frequently, each member undertakes the questioning on a particular area, one in which he is perhaps most competent, so you can expect each member to participate in the examination. Because time is limited, you may also expect some rather abrupt switches in the direction the questioning takes, so do not be upset by it. Normally, a board member will not pursue a single line of questioning unless he discovers a particular strength or weakness.

After each member has participated, the chairman will usually ask whether any member has any further questions, then will ask you if you have anything you wish to add. Unless you are expecting this question, it may floor you. Worse, it may start you off on an extended, extemporaneous speech. The board is not usually seeking more information. The question is principally to offer you a last opportunity to present further qualifications or to indicate that you have nothing to add. So, if you feel that a significant qualification or characteristic has been overlooked, it is proper to point it out in a sentence or so. Do not compliment the board on the thoroughness of their examination – they have been sketchy, and you know it. If you wish, merely say, "No thank you, I have nothing further to add." This is a point where you can "talk yourself out" of a good impression or fail to present an important bit of information. Remember, *you close the interview yourself*.

The chairman will then say, "That is all, Mr. _____, thank you." Do not be startled; the interview is over, and quicker than you think. Thank him, gather your belongings and take your leave. Save your sigh of relief for the other side of the door.

How to put your best foot forward

Throughout this entire process, you may feel that the board individually and collectively is trying to pierce your defenses, seek out your hidden weaknesses and embarrass and confuse you. Actually, this is not true. They are obliged to make an appraisal of your qualifications for the job you are seeking, and they want to see you in your best light. Remember, they must interview all candidates and a non-cooperative candidate may become a failure in spite of their best efforts to bring out his qualifications. Here are 15 suggestions that will help you:

1) Be natural – Keep your attitude confident, not cocky

If you are not confident that you can do the job, do not expect the board to be. Do not apologize for your weaknesses, try to bring out your strong points. The board is interested in a positive, not negative, presentation. Cockiness will antagonize any board member and make him wonder if you are covering up a weakness by a false show of strength.

2) Get comfortable, but don't lounge or sprawl

Sit erectly but not stiffly. A careless posture may lead the board to conclude that you are careless in other things, or at least that you are not impressed by the importance of the occasion. Either conclusion is natural, even if incorrect. Do not fuss with your clothing, a pencil or an ashtray. Your hands may occasionally be useful to emphasize a point; do not let them become a point of distraction.

3) Do not wisecrack or make small talk

This is a serious situation, and your attitude should show that you consider it as such. Further, the time of the board is limited – they do not want to waste it, and neither should you.

4) Do not exaggerate your experience or abilities

In the first place, from information in the application or other interviews and sources, the board may know more about you than you think. Secondly, you probably will not get away with it. An experienced board is rather adept at spotting such a situation, so do not take the chance.

5) If you know a board member, do not make a point of it, yet do not hide it

Certainly you are not fooling him, and probably not the other members of the board. Do not try to take advantage of your acquaintanceship – it will probably do you little good.

6) Do not dominate the interview

Let the board do that. They will give you the clues – do not assume that you have to do all the talking. Realize that the board has a number of questions to ask you, and do not try to take up all the interview time by showing off your extensive knowledge of the answer to the first one.

7) Be attentive

You only have 20 minutes or so, and you should keep your attention at its sharpest throughout. When a member is addressing a problem or question to you, give him your undivided attention. Address your reply principally to him, but do not exclude the other board members.

8) Do not interrupt

A board member may be stating a problem for you to analyze. He will ask you a question when the time comes. Let him state the problem, and wait for the question.

9) Make sure you understand the question

Do not try to answer until you are sure what the question is. If it is not clear, restate it in your own words or ask the board member to clarify it for you. However, do not haggle about minor elements.

10) Reply promptly but not hastily

A common entry on oral board rating sheets is "candidate responded readily," or "candidate hesitated in replies." Respond as promptly and quickly as you can, but do not jump to a hasty, ill-considered answer.

11) Do not be peremptory in your answers

A brief answer is proper – but do not fire your answer back. That is a losing game from your point of view. The board member can probably ask questions much faster than you can answer them.

12) Do not try to create the answer you think the board member wants

He is interested in what kind of mind you have and how it works – not in playing games. Furthermore, he can usually spot this practice and will actually grade you down on it.

13) Do not switch sides in your reply merely to agree with a board member

Frequently, a member will take a contrary position merely to draw you out and to see if you are willing and able to defend your point of view. Do not start a debate, yet do not surrender a good position. If a position is worth taking, it is worth defending.

14) Do not be afraid to admit an error in judgment if you are shown to be wrong

The board knows that you are forced to reply without any opportunity for careful consideration. Your answer may be demonstrably wrong. If so, admit it and get on with the interview.

15) Do not dwell at length on your present job

The opening question may relate to your present assignment. Answer the question but do not go into an extended discussion. You are being examined for a *new* job, not your present one. As a matter of fact, try to phrase ALL your answers in terms of the job for which you are being examined.

Basis of Rating

Probably you will forget most of these "do's" and "don'ts" when you walk into the oral interview room. Even remembering them all will not ensure you a passing grade. Perhaps you did not have the qualifications in the first place. But remembering them will help you to put your best foot forward, without treading on the toes of the board members.

Rumor and popular opinion to the contrary notwithstanding, an oral board wants you to make the best appearance possible. They know you are under pressure – but they also want to see how you respond to it as a guide to what your reaction would be under the pressures of the job you seek. They will be influenced by the degree of poise you display, the personal traits you show and the manner in which you respond.

ABOUT THIS BOOK

This book contains tests divided into Examination Sections. Go through each test, answering every question in the margin. At the end of each test look at the answer key and check your answers. On the ones you got wrong, look at the right answer choice and learn. Do not fill in the answers first. Do not memorize the questions and answers, but understand the answer and principles involved. On your test, the questions will likely be different from the samples. Questions are changed and new ones added. If you understand these past questions you should have success with any changes that arise. Tests may consist of several types of questions. We have additional books on each subject should more study be advisable or necessary for you. Finally, the more you study, the better prepared you will be. This book is intended to be the last thing you study before you walk into the examination room. Prior study of relevant texts is also recommended. NLC publishes some of these in our Fundamental Series. Knowledge and good sense are important factors in passing your exam. Good luck also helps. So now study this Passbook, absorb the material contained within and take that knowledge into the examination. Then do your best to pass that exam.

EXAMINATION SECTION

EXAMINATION SECTION
TEST 1

DIRECTIONS: Each question or incomplete statement is followed by several suggested answers or completions. Select the one that BEST answers the question or completes the statement. *PRINT THE LETTER OF THE CORRECT ANSWER IN THE SPACE AT THE RIGHT.*

NOTE: In balanced levers, as used in weighing devices, the basic principle is that the product of the force or weight acting on one arm multiplied by the distance of that force from the center of rotation must be equal to the product of the force or weight acting on the other arm multiplied by its distance from the center of rotation.

Questions 1-3.

DIRECTIONS: Questions 1 through 3, inclusive, are to be answered on the basis of the diagrams of balanced levers shown below. P is the center of rotation, W is the weight on the lever, F is the balancing force.

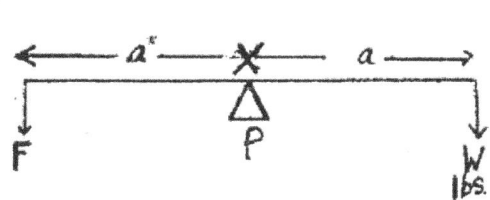
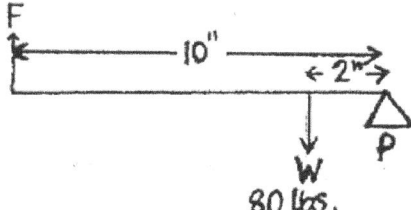

1. In Diagram 1, the force F required to balance the weight W lbs. on the lever shown is equal to _____ lbs.

   A. a/W B. W/a C. W D. Wa

   1.____

2. In Diagram 2, the force F required to balance the weight of 80 lbs. on the lever shown is _____ lbs.

   A. 4 B. 8 C. 16 D. 32

   2.____

3. The mechanical advantage of the lever shown in Diagram 2 is

   A. 4 B. 5 C. 8 D. 12

   3.____

4. Of the following, the MOST important reason for making counterpoise weights of hard durable metal is that

   A. the markings on the weights can be more easily read
   B. their weights are not likely to change much with use and there is greater accuracy in weighing operations
   C. they can be more easily tested by an inspector
   D. they can more easily be made to conform to permitted tolerances

   4.____

5. A platform scale in good working order is so constructed that a 1-lb. weight can balance 50 lbs. placed on the platform.
   If a load of 48 lbs. is placed on the platform and the scale balances when the alleged 1 lb. weight is used, then the actual weight of the balancing weight is MOST NEARLY. _____ lbs.

   A. .920   B. .960   C. 1.04   D. 1.06

6. The PRINCIPAL reason for the establishment of tolerances in the use of weighing and measuring devices is that

   A. it is extremely difficult to construct devices which will weigh or measure with absolute accuracy
   B. it saves time in carrying on weighing or measuring operations
   C. it simplifies the work of inspectors of weights and measures
   D. there are so many different types of weighing and measuring devices in use

7. The use of the simple straight face spring scale depends upon the principle that the stretch of the spring is

   A. dependent upon the material of which the weight acting on it is made
   B. different for identical weights acting on it
   C. directly proportional to the weight acting on it
   D. inversely proportional to the weight acting on it

8. Suppose that, in the part of a computing scale which shows the cost of the goods purchased, the indicating chart is divided into as many equal spaces per pound as the price per pound.
   If the price is 32 cents a pound and the indicator is at the end of the 8th space, the weight of the goods purchased is _____ ounces.

   A. 2   B. 4   C. 6   D. 8

9. The multiplication factor of a given scale is 33 1/3 to 1. If the load on the scale is 100 pounds, the weight required to counterbalance it is _____ pound(s).

   A. 1/3   B. 2/3   C. 3   D. 3 1/3

10. Of the following, the MOST likely reason why the metric system has NOT been widely adopted in the United States is that

    A. custom and long usage of other systems tend to prevent change to the metric system
    B. systems used in the United States are fixed by law
    C. the metric system is difficult to use in making ordinary calculations connected with weights and measures
    D. the metric system is useful in scientific work only

11. The Apothecaries' Weight system is MOST likely to be used by

    A. engineers   B. jewelers
    C. pharmacists   D. physicists

3 (#1)

12. The number of bushels in 128 pecks is 12.____

   A. 8 B. 32 C. 64 D. 256

13. The abbreviation *kw* stands for a unit used to measure 13.____

   A. cylindrical volume B. distance
   C. electric current D. power

14. If four rings each weigh 20 pennyweights, the one likely to contain the MOST gold is the one marked _____ karat. 14.____

   A. 10 B. 12 C. 14 D. 24

15. The LEAST accurate of the following statements is: 15.____

   A. Eight gills equals one pint
   B. One rod equals 5.5 yards
   C. The dram is used as a unit in both Apothecaries' Fluid Measure and Apothecaries' Weight
   D. The kilometer is equal to 1000 meters

16. The one of the following which is of MOST importance to a consumer of packaged goods is the 16.____

   A. gross weight B. net weight
   C. package size D. tare weight

17. The quality grades for canned fruits and vegetables are established by the 17.____

   A. Association of Official Agricultural Chemists
   B. National Bureau of Statistics
   C. City Health Code
   D. U.S. Department of Agriculture

18. The number of Fahrenheit degrees between the freezing point and boiling point of water is 18.____

   A. 32 B. 64 C. 100 D. 180

19. A micrometer is an instrument ordinarily used to measure very small 19.____

   A. densities B. thicknesses
   C. volumes D. weights

20. The drained weight of a can of vegetables refers to the weight of the 20.____

   A. contents after the liquid is poured off
   B. dry empty can
   C. liquid poured off
   D. wet empty can

21. Of the following, the one which is NOT considered kosher food during the Passover season is   21.____

   A. eggs
   B. fermented cereal products
   C. spices
   D. the forequarters of properly slaughtered lamb

22. The symbol B.T.U. stands for a unit of   22.____

   A. electricity   B. heat
   C. temperature   D. D, volume

23. The one of the following which is likely to be LEAST accurate when used as a measure of length is   23.____

   A. a tape made of steel
   B. a wooden yardstick with metal ends
   C. a yardstick covered with metal
   D. the distance between upholstery tacks driven into a store counter

24. The method used by an official grader to indicate the grade of a wholesale cut of beef is to   24.____

   A. place a cardboard tag bearing the grade name on the cut of beef
   B. place a metal tag bearing the grade name on the cut of beef
   C. stamp the grade name directly on the cut of beef
   D. use a harmless paste to attach a certificate bearing the grade name directly on the cut of beef

25. Of the following, the MOST accurate statement about the metric system is that   25.____

   A. it has no standards for dry measure
   B. it is a decimal system
   C. its units are based upon the number 12
   D. one kilometer in the metric system is approximately equal to one mile

KEY (CORRECT ANSWERS)

1. C
2. C
3. B
4. B
5. B

6. A
7. C
8. B
9. C
10. A

11. C
12. B
13. D
14. D
15. A

16. B
17. D
18. D
19. B
20. A

21. B
22. B
23. D
24. C
25. B

TEST 2

DIRECTIONS: Each question or incomplete statement is followed by several suggested answers or completions. Select the one that BEST answers the question or completes the statement. *PRINT THE LETTER OF THE CORRECT ANSWER IN THE SPACE AT THE RIGHT.*

1. The *cord*, the unit by which wood cut for fuel is commonly sold, is a unit of 1._____

   A. area   B. length   C. volume   D. weight

2. A thermostat is an instrument or device which functions as a result of changes in 2._____

   A. electric current
   B. speed of flow of a liquid
   C. speed of travel of a vehicle
   D. temperature

3. Coke is a type of 3._____

   A. liquid fuel additive
   B. liquid fuel derived from petroleum
   C. solid fuel derived from coal
   D. wood used for fuel

4. The abbreviation *ml* stands for 4._____

   A. mile   B. milliliter
   C. millimeter   D. million

5. The symbol > means is 5._____

   A. different from   B. greater than
   C. less than   D. the same as

6. An order to a person to appear in court at a certain time, as a witness, is known as a(n) 6._____

   A. affidavit   B. deposition
   C. injunction   D. subpoena

7. A *quire* is a unit used to indicate a certain 7._____

   A. length of cloth
   B. length of wire
   C. number of sheets of paper
   D. number of vegetables

8. The specific gravity of a liquid may be defined as the ratio of the weight of a given volume of the liquid to the weight of an equal volume of water. An empty bottle weighs 5 oz. When the bottle is filled with water, the total weight is 50 oz. When the bottle is filled with another liquid, the total weight is 95 oz. 8._____
   The specific gravity of the second liquid is MOST NEARLY

   A. .50   B. .58   C. 1.7   D. 2.0

9. If one inch is approximately equal to 2.54 centimeters, the number of inches in one meter is MOST NEARLY

   A. 14.2   B. 25.4   C. 39.4   D. 91.4

10. If there are 7680 minims in 1 pint and 128 fluid drams in 1 pint, the number of minims in a fluid dram is

    A. 30   B. 60   C. 120   D. 240

Questions 11-25.

DIRECTIONS: For each Question 11 through 25, inclusive, select the option whose meaning is MOST NEARLY the same as that of the capitalized word.

11. VARIATION
    A. change
    B. representative
    C. simplification
    D. trial

12. CREDIBLE
    A. believable
    B. impossible
    C. payable
    D. understandable

13. SUBTERFUGE
    A. argument   B. deception   C. excuse   D. flight

14. CONCISE
    A. brief   B. mixed   C. sarcastic   D. split

15. SPURIOUS
    A. angry   B. evident   C. false   D. odd

16. INCOHERENT
    A. damaged
    B. fearful
    C. inside
    D. uncoordinated

17. CORROBORATE
    A. confirm   B. confuse   C. decay   D. defraud

18. GRATUITY
    A. favor   B. greeting   C. scheme   D. tip

19. ALTERCATION
    A. angry dispute
    B. recent change
    C. renewal
    D. substitution

20. DISCRIMINATE
    A. involve in crime
    B. spread widely
    C. test repeatedly
    D. treat differently

21. DIVULGE
    A. reveal   B. separate   C. share   D. swell

22. EMBARGO
    A. container   B. license   C. load   D. D, stoppage

23. CENSURE
    A. anxiety   B. blame   C. middle   D. pause

24. CALIBRATE
    A. check someone else's calculations
    B. derive a formula to give desired results
    C. make calculations after inaccurate measurements have been taken
    D. mark appropriate graduations on a measuring instrument

25. ASCERTAIN
    A. authorize   B. determine   C. provide   D. publish

KEY (CORRECT ANSWERS)

1. C		11. A	
2. D		12. A	
3. C		13. B	
4. B		14. A	
5. B		15. C	
6. D		16. D	
7. C		17. A	
8. D		18. D	
9. C		19. A	
10. B		20. B	

21. A
22. D
23. B
24. D
25. D

TEST 3

DIRECTIONS: Each question or incomplete statement is followed by several suggested answers or completions. Select the one that BEST answers the question or completes the statement. *PRINT THE LETTER OF THE CORRECT ANSWER IN THE SPACE AT THE RIGHT.*

1. The number of liters in 836 pints is MOST NEARLY   1._____

   A. 104 B. 209 C. 395 D. 836

2. The number of cubic feet in a cubic yard is   2._____

   A. 3 B. 9 C. 27 D. 36

3. A cylindrical tank has inside dimensions as follows: height, 40 feet; diameter, 20 feet. Its volume is MOST NEARLY _____ x 3.1416 cubic feet.   3._____

   A. 800 B. 4000 C. 8000 D. 16000

4. There are approximately 67.2 cubic inches in a dry quart. If the number of cubic inches in a container is given, the method of finding the equivalent number of dry quarts is to   4._____

   A. divide the given number of cubic inches by 67.2
   B. divide the given number of cubic inches by 67.2 x 67.2 x 67.2
   C. multiply the given number of cubic inches by $\frac{11}{67.2} \times \frac{11}{67.2} \times \frac{11}{67.2}$
   D. multiply the given number of cubic inches by 67.2

5. An inspector wishes to test a weight used with a certain scale in a store. Using an accurate balance, he counterbalances with merchandise a standard weight equal to the weight of the merchandise. Then he substitutes the weight to be tested for the standard weight and determines any excess or deficiency, using small standard weights until equilibrium of the scale is again reached.
   This method is LIKELY to be   5._____

   A. *correct* because weights are permitted certain tolerances
   B. *correct* because the weight to be tested is being compared with standard weights
   C. *incorrect* because the small weights used by the inspector are likely to be less accurate than the large weights
   D. *incorrect* because the weight to be tested is substituted for a standard weight

6. An inspector is testing the volume of a glass graduate used by a pharmacist. He uses a standard graduate filled with water up to an appropriate mark and pours water from it into the graduate used by the pharmacist. When he reaches the same mark on the pharmacist's graduate, there is some water remaining in the standard graduate.
   Of the following, the MOST valid implication that can be made as a result of this test is that   6._____

   A. it cannot be considered a proper test since the marks on the pharmacist's graduate were made by the manufacturer
   B. it cannot be considered a proper test since water was used as the testing fluid
   C. the pharmacist's graduate, when used, is likely to deliver less than the amount indicated by the mark

D. the pharmacist's graduate, when used, is likely to deliver more than the amount indicated by the mark

7. Of the following, the one which is a basic purpose for the inspection of gasoline stations by the Department of Markets is to ensure that

   A. all the pumps used at the station are of the same type
   B. the consumer receives products as advertised according to brand, trade name, or quality
   C. the prices charged are the same as those in other stations in the vicinity
   D. the station is an official inspection station for the State Department of Motor Vehicles

7.____

8. Assume that you and another inspector are assigned to work together on a special project which will take several weeks to complete. You realize, after the first few days, that the other inspector is loafing on the job.
   Of the following, the MOST advisable action for you to take is to

   A. caution the other inspector that unless he does his share of the work, you will have to report the matter to your superior
   B. do as much of the work as you can and say nothing to the other employee or anyone else
   C. limit the amount of work you do to what you consider to be your proper share
   D. report the matter to your superior without further delay

8.____

9. Assume that you, as an inspector, disagree with the instructions of your supervisor as to the way a certain job should be done.
   Of the following, the MOST advisable action for you to take is to

   A. ask the supervisor to assign another inspector to do the work
   B. discuss the matter with your supervisor, giving your reasons for your disagreement with his instructions
   C. do the job according to your supervisor's instructions without making any comment
   D. do the job in your own way, if you feel that you can obtain proper results

9.____

10. An inspector entering a retail store finds that several boxes and merchandise displays are stacked near one of the scales used in the store. He tells the owner to move this material away from the scale.
    Of the following, the MOST probable reason for the inspector's action is that

    A. customers may be able to have a full view of the scale when making purchases
    B. customers may be detracted from watching the scale by the nearby displays
    C. material stored too near the scale may be pushed over by a customer and possibly injure other customers
    D. material stored too near the scale may possibly fall upon the scale and damage it

10.____

11. Of the following statements concerning reports prepared by an inspector, the one which is LEAST valid is:

    A. Prompt and accurate reports are of value to the work of the unit to which the inspector is assigned but they are of little concern to the operations of the rest of the department

11.____

B. Prompt and accurate reports may or may not impress superiors with the necessity for immediate action on their part
C. Reports prepared by inspectors may provide valuable reference material for future activities
D. Reports submitted by an inspector are useful indicators of the efficiency of his work

12. An inspector, after testing a scale in a retail market, finds that it gives short weight. The vendor promises to have the scale repaired immediately.
Of the following, the MOST advisable action for the inspector to take is to

    A. place a condemned tag on the scale in an inconspicuous spot so as not to embarrass the vendor
    B. place a condemned tag on the scale in such a way that anyone can easily see it
    C. recommend a good mechanic so that the scale can be properly repaired before he returns later that day
    D. tell the vendor that he will return later that day, and if the scale is repaired by then, he will take no further action

13. An inspector is in one of the retail markets supervised by the Department of Markets, He overhears a very loud argument going on between a customer and one of the vendors. The argument is concerned with the price being charged for some merchandise.
Of the following, the MOST advisable action for the inspector to take FIRST is to

    A. attempt to ignore the incident since he has nothing to do with prices being charged
    B. recommend that the vendor be charged with a violation for creating a disturbance in the market
    C. tell the patron to leave the market and make his purchase elsewhere if he can't keep quiet
    D. try to get the persons involved to settle the argument or quiet down

14. A certain person has made numerous complaints to the Department of Markets to the effect that he has been defrauded by various merchants with whom he has had dealings. In the past, investigation showed that none of his complaints were ever valid and that he is merely a *crank*. Assume that he has come to the office to make another complaint, and, since you happen to be one of the inspectors in the office at the time, you are told to interview him. From your conversation, it appears obvious to you that this is another baseless complaint.
Of the following, the MOST advisable action for you to take is to

    A. explain to him that there is no point in investigating this complaint since experience has shown that his complaints are always unfounded
    B. explain to him that unless he has specific evidence to support his complaint, the department will be unable to take any action
    C. tell him that the department will investigate this complaint as it does all others
    D. terminate the conversation abruptly and ignore the entire matter

4 (#3)

15. Suppose that the operator of a business licensed by the Department of Markets innocently commits a minor violation of one of the department's regulations.
Of the following, the MOST advisable action for an inspector to take is to

   A. consult his supervisor concerning the action that should be taken in such a case
   B. ignore the matter entirely
   C. make sure that the operator understands the appropriate action to take to prevent the recurrence of such violations in the future
   D. report the violation for appropriate penalty despite his feelings about the matter

15.____

16. Of the following statements concerning reports submitted by an Inspector of Markets, Weights, and Measures, the one which is MOST valid is:

   A. A very detailed report may be of less value than a brief report giving the essential facts
   B. Reports should be considered as confidential, and should be written in such language that they can be understood only by those who are technically trained in the work of the department
   C. Reports should give only the facts. Conclusions and recommendations should be left to the supervisor who reviews them.
   D. The position of the important points in a report will not have much influence on the emphasis placed on them by the reader as long as they are all included

16.____

17. Suppose that, as a newly appointed inspector, you are being given field training under the guidance of a supervising inspector. On a certain day, you have an appointment to meet him in the morning at a certain place of business, instead of at the office of the department. While coming from home, you are delayed a half hour on the subway. When you leave the subway station, which is some distance fron the meeting place, the MOST advisable action for you to take FIRST is to

   A. proceed as quickly as possible to the meeting place
   B. return directly to the office
   C. telephone the firm where you are to meet the supervising inspector and ask to speak to him
   D. telephone the office and explain the situation

17.____

18. The organization of the Department of Markets includes a bureau which has as one of its functions the gathering of information concerning the city's food supply and the prices of various items of food.
Of the following, the MOST important reason for this activity is that it

   A. can supply interested newspapers or other organizations with desired information
   B. may aid the public in securing proper nutrition at reasonable prices
   C. may supply needed information to producers and shippers of food
   D. supplies statistics which help give a complete picture of food distribution in the city

18.____

19. The time when an inspector should be especially watchful for possible short weighing by vendors in a supermarket is

   A. during early morning hours when there are likely to be few people in the store to see what is going on
   B. during employees' lunch hour periods when the manager of the store is not likely to be present

19.____

C. during evening rush hours when business is heavy and there are many people in the store
D. just before closing when the store is being prepared for the next day's business

Questions 20-21.

DIRECTIONS: Questions 20 and 21 are to be answered on the basis of the information contained in the following paragraph.

In all systems of weights and measures based on one or more arbitrary fundamental units, the concrete representation of the unit in the form of a standard is necessary, and the construction and preservation of such a standard is a matter of primary importance. Therefore, it is essential that the standard should be so constructed as to be as nearly permanent and invariable as human ingenuity can contrive. The reference of all measures to an original standard is essential for their correctness, and such a standard must be maintained and preserved in its integrity by some responsible authority which is thus able to provide against the use of false weights and measures. Accordingly, from earliest times, standards were constructed and preserved under the direction of kings and priests, and the temples were a favorite place for their deposit. Later, this duty was assumed by the government, and today, we find the integrity of standards of weights and measures safeguarded by international agreement.

20. Of the following, the MOST valid implication which can be made on the basis of the above paragraph is that   20.____

    A. fundamental units of systems of weights and measures should be represented by quantities so constructed that they are specific and constant
    B. in the earliest times standards were so constructed that they were as permanent and invariable as modern ones
    C. international agreement has practically relieved the U.S. government of the necessity of preserving standards of weights and measures
    D. the preservation of standards is of less importance than the ingenuity used in their construction

21. Of the following, the MOST appropriate title for the above passage is   21.____

    A. THE CONSTRUCTION AND PRESERVATION OF STANDARDS OF WEIGHTS AND MEASURES
    B. THE FIXING OF RESPONSIBILITY FOR THE ESTABLISHMENT OF STANDARDS OF WEIGHTS AND MEASURES
    C. THE HISTORY OF SYSTEMS OF WEIGHTS AND MEASURES
    D. THE VALUE OF PROPER STANDARDS IN PROVIDING CORRECT WEIGHTS AND MEASURES

Questions 22-23.

DIRECTIONS: Questions 22 and 23 are to be answered on the basis of the information contained in the following paragraph.

Accurate weighing and good scales insure that excess is not given just for the sake of good measure. No more striking example of the fundamental importance of correct weighing to the business man is found than in the simple and usual relation where a charge or value is obtained by multiplying a weight by a unit price. For example, a scale may weigh *light,* that is, the actual quantity delivered is in excess by 1 percent. The actual result is that the seller taxes himself. If his profit is supposed to be 10 percent of total sales, an overweight of 1 percent represents 10 percent of that profit. Under these conditions, the situation is as though the seller were required to pay a sales tax equivalent to what he is taxing himself.

22. Of the following, the MOST valid implication which can be made on the basis of the above paragraph is that 22.____

    A. consistent use of scales that weigh *light* will reduce sellers' profits
    B. no good businessman would give any buyer more than the weight required even if his scale is accurate
    C. the kind of situation described in the above passage could not arise if sales were being made of merchandise sold by the yard
    D. the use of incorrect scales is one of the reasons causing governments to impose sales taxes

23. According to the above paragraph, the MOST accurate of the following statements is: 23.____

    A. If his scale weighs *light* by an amount of 2 percent, the seller would deliver only 98 pounds when 100 pounds was the amount agreed upon
    B. If the seller's scale weighs *heavy,* the buyer will receive an amount in excess of what he intended to purchase
    C. If the seller's scale weighs *light* by an amount of 1 percent, a buyer who agreed to purchase 50 pounds of merchandise would actually receive 50J pounds
    D. The use of a scale which delivers an amount which is in excess of that required is an example of deliberate fraud

Questions 24-25.

DIRECTIONS: Questions 24 and 25 are to be answered on the basis of the information contained in the following passage.

Food shall be deemed to be misbranded:

1. If its labeling is false or misleading in any particular.

2. If any word, statement or other information required by or under authority of this article to appear on the label or labeling is not prominently placed thereon with such conspicuousness (as compared with other words, statements, designs or devices in the labeling) and in such terms as to render it likely to be read and understood by the ordinary individual under customary conditions of purchase and use.

3. If it purports to be or is represented as a food for which a standard of quality has been prescribed and its quality falls below such standard, unless its label bears a statement that it falls below such standard.

24. According to the above passage, the MOST accurate of the following statements is: 24.____
    A. A food may be considered misbranded if the label contains a considerable amount of information which is not required
    B. If a consumer purchased one type of canned food although he intended to buy another, the food is probably misbranded
    C. If a food is used in large amounts by a group of people of certain foreign origin, it can be considered misbranded unless the label is in the foreign language with which they are familiar
    D. The required information on a label is likely to be in larger print than other information which may appear on it

25. According to the above passage, the one of the following foods which may be considered 25.____
to be misbranded is a
    A. can of peaches with a label which carries the brand name of the packer but states *Below Standard in Quality*
    B. can of vegetables with a label on which is printed a shield which states *U.S. Grade B*
    C. package of frozen food which has some pertinent information printed on it in very small type which a customer cannot read and which the store manager cannot read when asked to do so by the customer
    D. package of margarine of the same size as the usual package of butter, kept near the butter, but clearly labeled as margarine

KEY (CORRECT ANSWERS)

1. C		11. A	
2. C		12. B	
3. B		13. D	
4. A		14. B	
5. B		15. C	
6. C		16. A	
7. B		17. C	
8. A		18. B	
9. B		19. C	
10. A		20. A	

21. D
22. A
23. C
24. D
25. C

TEST 4

DIRECTIONS: Each question or incomplete statement is followed by several suggested answers or completions. Select the one that BEST answers the question or completes the statement. *PRINT THE LETTER OF THE CORRECT ANSWER IN THE SPACE AT THE RIGHT.*

Questions 1-8.

DIRECTIONS: Questions 1 through 8, inclusive, are based SOLELY on Tables A and B and the notes below.

TABLE A
PURCHASES MADE IN A MEAT MARKET
(Self-Service Refrigerated Meat Case)

ITEM	PRINTED PRICE PER POUND	WEIGHT INDICATED	ACTUAL WEIGHT	PRICE PER PACKAGE
Beef Liver	40¢	1 lb. 2 oz.	1 lb. 2 oz.	50¢
Pork Loins:				
Rib End	29¢	2 lbs. 4 oz.	2 lbs. 1 oz.	66¢
Loin End	32¢	1 lb. 8 oz.	1 lb. 5 oz.	48¢
Veal Chops:				
Shoulder	70¢	2 lbs. 8 oz.	2 lbs. 2 oz.	$1.75
Rib	80¢	1 lb. 10 oz.	1 lb. 12 oz.	$1.50
Loin	90¢	3 lbs. 2 oz.	2 lbs. 10 oz.	$2.05
Flank Steak	88¢	2 lbs. 14 oz.	2 lbs. 3 oz.	$2.53
Cube Steak	80¢	12 oz.	12 oz.	60¢
Top Sirloin Roast	99¢	1 lb. 12 oz.	1 lb. 8 oz.	$1.75
Fresh Ham	55¢	4 lbs. 6 oz.	4 lbs.	$2.40
Bologna	40¢	6 oz.	5 oz.	15¢
Frankfurters	45¢	1 lb, 4 oz.	1 lb. 1 oz.	57¢

TABLE B
PURCHASES MADE IN A CONFECTIONERY

| ITEM | PRICE QUOTED PER POUND | AMOUNT REQUESTED | WEIGHTS USED | | | | | PRICE CHARGD |
			2 lb.	1 lb.	1/2 lb.	1/4 lb.	1 oz.	
Chocolate Almonds	$1.12	3 1/4 lbs.	1	1		1	–	$3.64
Peanut Brittle	$1.09	1 3/4 lbs.	–	1	1	1	–	$1.91
Bridge Mix	$1.25	5 oz.				1	1	$ .40
Special TV Mix	$1.49	2 1/2 lbs.	1	–	1	–	–	$3.75
Choc. Cherries	$1.89	40 pieces	1			1	3	$4.60
Caramels	$1.05	4 lbs.	2	–	–	–	–	$4.20
Cashew Crunch	$1.04	7 lbs.	2	2	1	2	–	$7.28

NOTES

Tables A and B represent hypothetical purchases made in a meat market and in a confectionery. In the case of the meat market, the price and weight figures were taken from the label on each meat package. The label gives the price per pound, the supposed weight of the package, and the price of the package. In answering questions pertaining to the meat market, make no allowance for the weight of wrapping materials.

2 (#4)

At the confectionery, all sales are weighed out on an even-balance scale using weights of various sizes. In checking the accuracy of the weights, it was found that the 1 oz. weights did actually weigh 1 oz. each, but that the 1/4 lb. weights weighed 3 oz. each, the 1/2 lb. weights weighed 6 oz. each, the 1 lb. weights weighed 14 oz. each, and the 2 lb. weights weighed 1 lb. 10 oz. each. While the confectionery purchases were being made, note was taken of the weights used in weighing each purchase. The weights which were used are shown in Table B.

If you find, when computing the proper price of a meat or candy item, that the price comes out to a fractional part of a penny, assume that the proprietor is justified in charging a sum equal to the next higher penny. For example, if the computed price of an article is 38 1/4 cents, the proprietor may properly charge 39 cents.

1. If the weight indicated on the package containing veal chops (loin) were accurate, the cost of the package should have been

   A. $2.36   B. $2.75   C. $2.79   D. $2.82

2. Based on the actual weight, how much should the package of bologna have cost?

   A. 13¢   B. 14¢   C. 16¢   D. 17¢

3. The purchaser who bought the flank steak package overpaid, on the basis of the actual weight of the package, APPROXIMATELY

   A. 9¢   B. 53¢   C. 60¢   D. 69¢

4. The actual weight of all of the packages of meat shown in Table A is _____ lbs. _____ oz.

   A. 20; 8
   B. 20; 13
   C. 23; 8
   D. none of the above

5. Each chocolate cherry actually weighs APPROXIMATELY _____ oz.

   A. .2   B. .5   C. .8   D. 1.2

6. The cashew crunch purchase actually weighted _____ lbs. _____ oz.

   A. 5; 9   B. 5; 12   C. 5; 15   D. D, 6; 2

7. In accordance with the amount actually received, the chocolate almond purchase should have cost MOST NEARLY

   A. $2.31   B. $2.67   C. $2.80   D. $3.01

8. Which of the following combinations of weights used by the confectionery would have come CLOSEST to giving the purchaser of the Special TV Mix the weight he requested? 1-2 lb. weight; _____.

   A. 1 1/2 lb. weight
   B. 2 1/2 lb. weight
   C. 2 1/2 lb. weights; 1-1 oz. weight
   D. 2 1/2 lb. weights; 21 oz. weights

Questions 9-10.

DIRECTIONS: Questions 9 and 10 are to be answered on the basis of the information contained in the following paragraph.

Open Air Markets originally came into existence spontaneously when groups of pushcart peddlers congregated in spots where business was good. Good business induced them to return to these spots daily, and, thus, unofficial open air markets arose. These peddlers paid no fees, and the city received no revenue from them. Confusion and disorder reigned in these unsupervised markets; the earliest arrivals secured the best locations, unless or until forcibly ejected by stronger or tougher peddlers. Although the Open Air Markets supplied a definite need in the community, there were many detrimental factors involved in their operation. They were unsightly, created unsanitary conditions in market streets by the deposit of garbage and waste and were a definite obstruction to traffic, as well as a fire hazard.

9. On the basis of the above paragraph, the MOST accurate of the following statements is: 9.____

    A. Each peddler in the original open air markets had his own fixed location
    B. Open air markets were originally organized by means of agreements between groups of pushcart peddlers
    C. The locations of these markets depended upon the amount of business the vendors were able to do
    D. There was confusion and disorder in these open air markets because the peddlers were not required to pay any fees to the city

10. Of the following, the MOST valid implication which can be made on the basis of the above paragraph is that the 10.____

    A. detrimental aspect of the operations of open air markets was the probable reason for the creation of enclosed markets under the supervision of the Department of Markets
    B. open air markets could not supply any community need without proper supervision
    C. original open air markets were good examples of the operation of fair competition in business
    D. possibility of obtaining a source of revenue was probably the most important reason for the city's ultimate undertaking of the supervision of open air markets

Questions 11-12.

DIRECTIONS: Questions 11 and 12 are to be answered on the basis of the information contained in the following paragraph.

A person who displays on his window, door, or in his place of business, words or letters in Hebraic characters other than the word *kosher,* or any sign, emblem, insignia, six-pointed star, symbol or mark in simulation of same, without displaying in conjunction therewith in English letters of at least the same size as such characters, signs, emblems, insignia or marks, the words *we sell kosher meat and food only,* or *we sell non-kosher meat and food only,* or *we sell both kosher and non-kosher meat and food,* as the case may be, is guilty of a misdemeanor. Possession of non-kosher meat and food in any place of business advertising the sale of kosher meat and food only is presumptive evidence that the person in possession exposes the same for sale with intent to defraud, in violation of the provisions of this section.

11. Of the following, the MOST valid implication that can be made on the basis of the above paragraph is that a person who 11.____

A. displays on his window, a six-pointed star in addition to the word *kosher* in Hebraic letters is guilty of intent to defraud
B. displays on his window the word *kosher* in Hebraic characters intends to indicate that he has only kosher food for sale
C. sells both kosher and non-kosher food in the same place of business is guilty of a misdemeanor
D. sells only that type of food which can be characterized as neither kosher nor non-kosher, such as fruit and vegetables, without an explanatory sign in English, is guilty of intent to defraud

12. Of the following, the one which would constitute a violation of the rules of the above paragraph is a case in which a person   12.____

    A. displays the word *kosher* on his window in Hebraic letters, has only kosher meat and food in the store but has some non-kosher meat in the rear of the establishment
    B. selling both kosher and non-kosher meat and food uses words in Hebraic letters, other than the word *kosher*, on his window and a sign of the same sized letters in English stating, *we sell both kosher and non-kosher meat and food*
    C. selling only kosher meat and food uses words in Hebraic letters, other than the word *kosher*, on his window and a sign of the same sized letters in English stating, *we sell kosher meat and food only*
    D. selling only non-kosher meat and food displays a six-pointed star on his window and a sign of the same sized letters in English stating, *we sell only non-kosher meat and food*

Questions 13-14.

DIRECTIONS: Questions 13 and 14 are to be answered on the basis of the information contained in the following paragraph.

COMMODITIES IN GLASS BOTTLES OR JARS

The contents of the bottle may be stated in terms of weight or of fluid measure, the weight being indicated in terms of pounds and ounces and the fluid measure being indicated in terms of gallons, quarts, pints, half-pints, gills or fluid ounces. When contents are liquid, the amount should not be stated in terms of weight. The marking indicating content is to be on a tag attached to the bottle or upon a label. The letters shall be in bold-faced type at least one-ninth of an inch (1/9") in height for bottles or jars having a capacity of a gill, half-pint, pint or multiples of a pint, and letters at least three-sixteenths of an inch (3/16") in height for bottles of other capacities, on a part of the tag or label free from other printing or ornamentation, leaving a clear space around the marking which indicates the contents.

13. Of the following, the one which does NOT meet the requirements of the above paragraph is a

   A. bottle of cooking oil with a label stating *contents -16 fluid ounces* in appropriate sized letters
   B. bottle of vinegar with a label stating *contents - 8 ounces avoir* in appropriate sized letters
   C. glass jar filled with instant coffee with a label stating *contents - 1 lb. S oz. avoir* in appropriate sized letters
   D. glass jar filled with liquid bleach with a label stating *contents - 1 quart* in appropriate sized letters

14. Of the following, the one which does meet the requirements of the above paragraph is a

   A. bottle filled with a low-calorie liquid sweetner with a label stating *contents - S fluid ounces* in letters 1/12" high
   B. bottle filled with ammonia solution for cleaning with a label stating *contents - 1 pint* in letters 1/10" high
   C. jar filled with baking powder with a label stating *contents - 1/2 pint* in letters 1/4" high
   D. jar filled with hard candy with a label stating *contents - 1 lb. avoir* in letters 1/2" high

Question 15.

DIRECTIONS: Question 15 is to be answered on the basis of the information contained in the following passage.

DEALERS IN SECOND HAND DEVICES

1. It shall be unlawful for any person to engage in or conduct the business of dealing in, trading in, selling, receiving, or repairing condemned, rebuilt or used weighing or measuring devices without a permit therefor.

2. Such permit shall expire on the twenty-eighth day of February next succeeding the date of issuance thereof.

3. Every person engaged in the above business, within five days after the making of a repair, or the sale and delivery of a repaired, rebuilt or used weighing or measuring device, shall serve notice in writing on the commissioner giving the name and address of the person for whom the repair has been made or to whom a repaired, rebuilt or used weighing or measuring device has been sold or delivered, and shall include a statement that such device has been so altered, repaired, or rebuilt as to conform to the regulations of the department.

15. According to the above passage, the MOST accurate of the following statements is:

   A. A permit issued to engage in the business mentioned above, first issued on April 23, 2015, expired on February 29, 2016
   B. A rebuilt or repaired weighing or measuring device should not operate with less error than the tolerances permitted by the regulations of the department
   C. If a used scale in good condition is sold, it is not necessary for the seller to notify the commissioner of the name and address of the buyer

D. There is a difference in the time required to notify the commissioner of a repair or of a sale of a repaired device

Questions 16-17,

DIRECTIONS: Questions 16 and 17 are to be answered on the basis of the information contained in the following passage.

(a) It shall be unlawful for any person, firm or corporation to sell or offer for sale at retail for use in internal combustion engines in motor vehicles any gasoline unless such seller shall post and keep continuously posted on the individual pump or other dispensing device from which such gasoline is sold or offered for sale a sign or placard not less than seven inches in height and eight inches in width nor larger than twelve inches in height and twelve inches in width and stating clearly in numbers of uniform size the selling price or prices per gallon of such gasoline so sold or offered for sale from such pump or other dispensing device.

(b) The amount of governmental tax to be collected in connection with the sale of such gasoline shall be stated on such sign or placard and separately and apart from such selling price or prices.

16. The one of the following price signs posted on a gasoline pump which would be in violation of the above passage is a sign _____ square inches in size and _____ inches high.

   A. 144; 12
   B. 84; 7
   C. 72; 12
   D. 60; 8

17. According to the above passage, the LEAST accurate of the following statements is:

   A. Gasoline may be sold from a dispensing device other than a pump
   B. If two different pumps are used to sell the same grade of gasoline, a price sign must appear on each pump
   C. The amount of governmental tax and the price of the gasoline must not be stated on the same sign
   D. The sizes of the numbers used on a sign to indicate the price of gasoline must be the same

18. Although the Live Poultry Law requires that live poultry be sold at the Live Poultry Terminal according to grade, it has been said that such grading is not truly necessary for the business carried on there.
    Of the following, the MOST probable reason for this statement is that

   A. it is extremely difficult to determine the grades of live poultry since there are so many factors to be considered in making a determination
   B. supply and demand will determine prices paid by the merchants and dealers operating there and good poultry will naturally bring the highest prices whether it is officially graded or not
   C. the differences between the various grades of live poultry are likely to be so small that they are of little consequence to the ultimate consumer
   D. the standards for grades of live poultry will tend to differ in different parts of the country, and this would lead to confusion when grading is involved in wholesale dealings in poultry

19. Under the Live Poultry Law, a *Commission Merchant* is defined as: *A person in the business of receiving live poultry from shippers, farmers, producers or others on consignment for sale on their behalf.*
Of the following, the MOST valid assumption that can be made on the basis of the above definition is that the commission merchant

    A. is considered to be the owner of any live poultry he sells at the Live Poultry Terminal and returns part of his profit to the shipper, farmer or producer
    B. must guarantee a certain return to the shipper, farmer or producer
    C. must necessarily receive only a fixed percentage of the sales he is able to make at the Live Poultry Terminal
    D. probably makes agreements with shippers, farmers and producers as to how he shall be paid for his services

19.____

20. The regulations of the Live Poultry Law contain restrictions against the feeding of live poultry at the Live Poultry Terminal before sale.
Of the following, the MOST probable reason for such regulations is that

    A. at the terminal it is difficult to maintain the proper sanitary conditions under which poultry should be fed
    B. such feeding would probably result in an increase in weight for which the buyer would pay without receiving proper value for his purchase
    C. the time involved in feeding the poultry would delay transactions at the terminal and interfere with its efficient operation
    D. those who do business at the terminal may not be familiar with the proper type of feed for the poultry and the physical condition of the birds may be affected

20.____

21. One of the functions of the inspectors at the Live Poultry Terminal is to examine the poultry to see that any birds affected by disease are not offered for sale or sold.
Of the following, the PRINCIPAL reason for such inspection is to

    A. influence shippers, farmers, and producers to take proper measures to prevent poultry from becoming diseased
    B. protect the buyer at the terminal from losing money through the purchase of diseased poultry which he may not be able to resell
    C. protect the seller from being accused of offering unfit poultry for sale
    D. protect the ultimate consumer from purchasing poultry which is unfit for human consumption

21.____

22. It shall be unlawful for any person to deal in, receive, buy, sell, give away, distribute or have in his possession dressed poultry which has been processed outside of the city unless such poultry has received ante-mortem inspection and has been approved for condition by the United States Department of Agriculture or the State Department of Agriculture and Markets.
The term *ante-mortem inspection,* as used in the above passage, refers to inspection

    A. after slaughter
    B. before slaughter
    C. by a governmental agency
    D. by the processing plant operator

22.____

23. A squab is a young

　　A. female duck　　　　　　　　B. goose of either sex
　　C. pigeon of either sex　　　　D. tom turkey

24. The one of the following classes of chickens which is youngest in age is a

　　A. broiler　　B. cock　　C. fowl　　D. roaster

25. The guinea is a type of

　　A. duck
　　B. goose
　　C. turkey
　　D. poultry different from any of those mentioned above

KEY (CORRECT ANSWERS)

1.	D	11.	B
2.	A	12.	A
3.	C	13.	B
4.	B	14.	D
5.	C	15.	A
6.	B	16.	C
7.	D	17.	C
8.	D	18.	B
9.	C	19.	D
10.	A	20.	B

21. D
22. B
23. C
24. A
25. D

EXAMINATION SECTION
TEST 1

DIRECTIONS: Each question or incomplete statement is followed by several suggested answers or completions. Select the one that BEST answers the question or completes the statement. *PRINT THE LETTER OF THE CORRECT ANSWER IN THE SPACE AT THE RIGHT.*

1. Assume that you are making a regular inspection in a store a few days before Christmas. The store owner hands you a small, wrapped package, saying it is a Christmas gift for your family.
   Of the following, it would be BEST for you to

   A. accept the gift since it is small
   B. accept the gift since you do not want to hurt the owner's feelings
   C. explain to the owner that you cannot accept the gift, because it would be against departmental regulations
   D. tell the owner that you cannot accept the gift because you have none to give him in return

   1.____

2. Suppose you overhear a conversation in the street between two women regarding illegal sales practices in a nearby electric appliance store. The one of the following that you should do FIRST is

   A. identify yourself to the women and urge them to file a complaint
   B. act the role of an innocent bystander and urge them to file a complaint
   C. make an inspection of the establishment in question
   D. report the incident to your supervisor

   2.____

3. Assume that you are on a 9 A.M. to 5 P.M. shift. On a particular Monday you have scheduled an area survey for businesses operating without a license. When you arrive at work that day, you are given a directive from the Commissioner assigning you to a special project effective that day.
   The one of the following that you should do is to

   A. carry out the special project as described in the directive
   B. perform the scheduled survey and then report for the special project
   C. tell your supervisor to assign another inspector to the special project until you have finished the survey
   D. work on the special project during regular working hours and perform your survey after hours

   3.____

4. Assume that you receive a telephone call from a person who explains that he is thinking of shopping in a particular store and wants to know if that store has ever been issued any violations by your department. In accordance with department policy, you should

   A. check the department records and give him the correct information
   B. politely explain why you cannot give out that information
   C. state that the store has never been given a violation
   D. mail him a copy of the inspection records for that store

   4.____

5. You are assigned to make inspections before 9 A.M., the usual start of your working day. At approximately 9 A.M., you are required to call your supervisor, giving the names, locations, and types of the inspected premises.
The one of the following which offers the BEST explanation for this procedure is that it

   A. keeps the supervisor informed of the whereabouts of his subordinates
   B. assures that inspections are effective
   C. protects the business from being unnecessarily re-inspected
   D. verifies that the inspector was working and not claiming time not actually worked

6. Assume that you have just completed the inspection of a business when the owner approaches you and explains that a community organization of which he is a member is upset over the large number of unlicensed itinerant peddlers in the neighborhood. He asks whether you can do anything about the situation.
Under these circumstances, it would be BEST for you to

   A. add the complaint to your work schedule and investigate it according to standard procedure
   B. advise the owner that the department is aware of the problem and will investigate it as soon as possible
   C. explain that you may act only on written complaints
   D. tell the owner that you will bring his complaint to the attention of your supervisor

7. A department regulation states that when advertising a piece of merchandise as *free* upon the purchase of another item, the price for the purchased item shall not be increased over its regular price.
The BEST reason for this regulation is that it

   A. permits the department to control the number of *free* offers that a store operator can advertise
   B. permits the retailer to maintain inventory records of the number of special items purchased
   C. protects consumers from paying for any portion of the cost of the *free* item through the increased price of the purchased item
   D. saves time for the retailer who might otherwise have to reprice all items

8. A reporter asks whether he may accompany you for a few hours to gather information for a newspaper story. According to departmental policy, you should

   A. accede to his request
   B. let him join you, but only for a short time
   C. suggest that he come back another day when you will have had time to arrange an inspection route with more interesting problems
   D. explain that he must arrange such a tour through the department's public relations office

9. Suppose you are making an inspection to determine whether there are any violations of the laws, rules, and regulations governing itinerant peddlers. The one of the following that you should do FIRST is to

   A. check for a peddler's license
   B. identify yourself

C. make a test purchase
D. visit businesses in the area selling similar merchandise

10. Department regulations prohibit a door-to-door salesman from gaining a potential customer's attention by claiming that he is taking a survey or distributing free gifts. The BEST reason for this law is to

    A. prevent anyone from taking surveys or distributing free gifts
    B. protect consumers from salesmen working under false pretenses
    C. protect salesmen from consumers who take free gifts but have no intention of purchasing anything
    D. put door-to-door salesmen out of business

11. When a retailer plans to offer for sale thawed meat or fish, he is required by department regulations to do which one of the following?

    A. Label the product *thawed* or *defrosted*
    B. Reduce the price of the product
    C. Refreeze the product and label it *refrozen*
    D. Remove the unsold portion from sale within three hours

12. Certain perishable foods must be stamped, printed, or otherwise plainly and conspicuously marked with either the last day or date of sale or the last day or date of recommended usage. Among these foods are

    A. bread, meat, and poultry
    B. bread, milk, and meat
    C. eggs, bread, and milk
    D. eggs, milk, and poultry

13. According to Department regulations, hamburger offered for sale should NOT contain more than _____ fat.

    A. 10%   B. 20%   C. 30%   D. 40%

14. All information required by Department regulations to appear on a container MUST appear in

    A. black ink on a white background
    B. letters at least one inch high
    C. the English language
    D. two different languages on the container

15. All commodities offered for sale in a container must, according to Department regulations, include on the outside or top of the container all of the following EXCEPT a

    A. declaration of the identity of the commodity, unless it can be easily identified through the container
    B. declaration of the name and address of the retailer
    C. declaration of the name of the manufacturer, packer or distributor
    D. declaration of the net quantity

4 (#1)

16. According to Department regulations, whenever meat is packaged by a retailer in advance of being sold, which one of the following MUST also be provided, not more than 30 feet from the display counter?
A(n)

   A. chart indicating the date the item must be removed from sale
   B. chart indicating the date the item was first placed on sale
   C. means of testing the item for adulteration
   D. accurate computing scale marked *for customer use* or a sign telling customers where such scale is located

16.____

17. According to Department regulations, retail stores are NOT permitted to sell prepackaged meat unless the package is

   A. colorless and transparent
   B. less than one ounce in weight
   C. of a heat-resistant material
   D. open at one end

17.____

18. Hamburger meat may contain all of the following EXCEPT

   A. chemical preservatives B. added fat
   C. chuck steak   D. neck meat

18.____

19. The net weight declaration on a package of food MUST be

   A. in grams as well as ounces
   B. near the top of the package
   C. on the label but in no specific place
   D. on the main panel of the label

19.____

20. The fat content of oleomargarine MUST be at least _____ percent.

   A. 40   B. 60   C. 80   D. 90

20.____

21. Retail gasoline stations are required by Department regulations to do all of the following EXCEPT

   A. have on the premises an approved 5 gallon test measure
   B. prime each pump before serving the public every day
   C. test the accuracy of each pump every day
   D. test the gasoline for adulteration every day

21.____

22. According to Department regulations, which of the following is TRUE of computing gasoline pumps NOT equipped with an *interlock device*?
They

   A. are permitted only by special permission of the Commissioner
   B. are permitted only if they have the following statement on the face of dial: *Gallons and sales indications must be at zero when delivery is begun*
   C. can be used only in gasoline stations with gross receipts of less than $50,000 per year
   D. cannot be used under any circumstances

22.____

5 (#1)

23. According to Department regulations, vehicle tanks for delivery of fuel oil shall be provided with a device adjacent to the meter inlet to insure that only fuel oil goes through the meter. This device is known as a(n) 23.____

    A. bypass
    B. pre-measurement meter
    C. true-volume regulator
    D. air eliminator

24. Generally, no person may be licensed by the Department unless he is a citizen of the United States or 24.____

    A. has filed a declaration of intention of becoming a citizen
    B. has received special written permission from the Commissioner
    C. is licensed by the country of which he is a citizen
    D. maintains his legal residence in the country of which he is a citizen

25. Laundries licensed by the Department are prohibited from doing which one of the following? 25.____

    A. Advertising
    B. Charging fees based on weight of the laundry
    C. Employing people who are not citizens of the United States
    D. Remaining open on Sunday

26. All applicants for laundry licenses are required to be investigated by an inspector to determine whether or not the laundry will 26.____

    A. be detrimental to the health of those living or employed in the immediate vicinity
    B. employ women
    C. present unfair competition to other laundries which are already established in the neighborhood
    D. use the most up-to-date equipment

27. Sightseeing guides licensed by the Department are prohibited from doing all of the following EXCEPT 27.____

    A. accepting a commission from a common show operator for bringing a sightseeing group to his theater
    B. selling tickets on the street for sightseeing tours
    C. selling tickets within 50 feet of a licensed sightseeing ticket office
    D. taking a group of people to a museum or other point of interest where a fee is charged

28. Theater licensees are required by Department regulations to display conspicuously a notice in the box office when a movie is 28.____

    A. appropriate for children
    B. in a language other than English
    C. more than one year old
    D. more than two hours in length

29. According to the Consumer Protection Law, once a person has signed a contract for home improvement, which of the following is TRUE? 29.____
    The contract can

A. be cancelled within three days
B. be cancelled within ten days
C. be cancelled within two weeks
D. not be cancelled

30. The MAXIMUM fee which a licensed employment agency is allowed to charge for placing a person in a job is based on the

    A. age of the employee
    B. length of time the employee has been out of work
    C. length of time the job has been vacant
    D. salary of the job

31. Mail order sellers must deliver or mail, make a refund, or notify the customer of any delay within

    A. two weeks B. six weeks
    C. two months D. six months

32. All of the following Department regulations apply to licensed public porters EXCEPT

    A. they are not permitted to work on Sundays or legal holidays
    B. they may not demand payment in excess of that allowed by the Department
    C. they may not refuse to transport articles unless they are already otherwise employed
    D. while working they must wear the badge issued to them by the Department

33. Department regulations prohibit minors under 16 years of age from entering a licensed billiard room unless

    A. alcoholic beverages are specifically prohibited from the establishment
    B. they are accompanied by a parent or guardian
    C. they are employed by the establishment
    D. they are playing billiards

34. The Truth-In-Pricing Regulations apply to

    A. all retail establishments which sell food
    B. only those retail establishments whose annual volume of business is over two million dollars
    C. only those retail establishments whose annual volume of business is over ten million dollars
    D. only those retail establishments whose annual volume is over fifty million dollars

35. The MAXIMUM amount of money in disputes that can be decided by the small claims courts of the city is

    A. $1,000 B. $1,500 C. $2,000 D. $3,000

KEY (CORRECT ANSWERS)

1. C
2. D
3. A
4. A
5. D

6. D
7. C
8. D
9. C
10. B

11. A
12. C
13. C
14. C
15. B

16. D
17. A
18. A
19. D
20. C

21. D
22. B
23. D
24. A
25. D

26. A
27. D
28. B
29. A
30. D

31. B
32. A
33. B
34. B
35. D

TEST 2

DIRECTIONS: Each question or incomplete statement is followed by several suggested answers or completions. Select the one that BEST answers the question or completes the statement. *PRINT THE LETTER OF THE CORRECT ANSWER IN THE SPACE AT THE RIGHT.*

1. A certain store is selling cloth table napkins. The small size cost 35¢ each or 99¢ for a package of 3. The large size cost 55¢ each or $1.59 for a package of 3. The LOWEST possible price for 11 large napkins and 10 small ones is

   A. $4.03   B. $8.99   C. $9.19   D. $11.13

2. Children's sweaters were sold in a certain store for $13.95 each. They were then placed on sale at 40% off. If a woman bought 3 sweaters on sale and was charged $24.11 (excluding sales tax), she was

   A. charged the correct price
   B. overcharged $7.37
   C. undercharged $1.00
   D. undercharged $17.74

3. Assume you check the weight of all the packages of meat in a certain supermarket. Of the 585 packages tested, 40% are shortweight. Of the shortweight packages, 15% are shortweight by 10% or more.
   The number of packages of meat that are shortweight by 10% or more is MOST NEARLY

   A. 22   B. 23   C. 25   D. 52

4. A certain car rental agency charges $9.00 a day and 10¢ a mile, but gives a 15% discount to anyone renting a car for 1 week or more. If one man rents a car for 3 days and drives 375 miles, and another man rents a car for 9 days and drives 775 miles, the total cost for the two rentals will be MOST NEARLY

   A. $78.28   B. $199.00   C. $201.70   D. $223.00

5. Of the 435 boxes of Brand X cookies on the shelves in a certain supermarket, 31% are more than 5% shortweight. Of the remaining boxes, 18% weigh over 5% more than they should.
   The number of boxes that fall within 5% of the correct weight is MOST NEARLY

   A. 164   B. 213   C. 222   D. 246

6. The total area of the diagram is
   A. 375 square feet
   B. 400 square feet
   C. 44 square yards
   D. 125 square yards

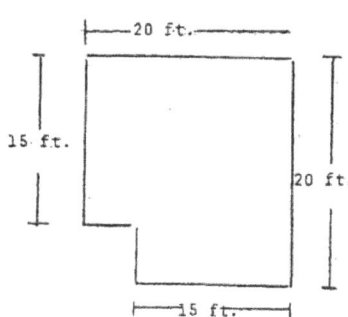

7. If the area of the floor plan diagrammed is 210 square feet, the length of side A is _____ feet.
   A. 3
   B. 5
   C. 7 1/2
   D. 10

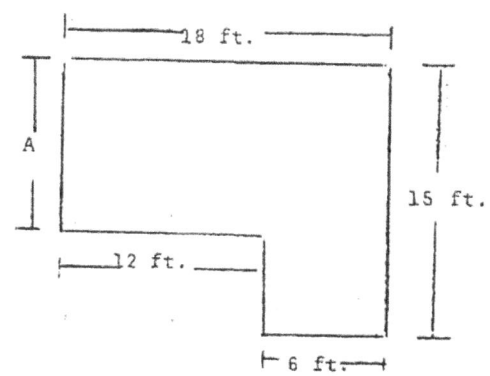

8. In a unit of five Inspectors, one Inspector makes an average of 12 inspections a day, two Inspectors make an average of 10 inspections a day, and two Inspectors make an average of 9 inspections a day. If in a certain week one of the Inspectors who makes an average of nine inspections a day is out of work on Monday and Tuesday because of illness and all the Inspectors do no inspections for half a day on Wednesday because of a special meeting, the number of inspections this unit can be expected to make in that week is MOST NEARLY

   A. 215   B. 225   C. 230   D. 250

9. In dress and appearance, an Inspector should
   A. dress in a somewhat sloppy way to disarm a merchant into thinking you are not efficient
   B. make no special effort but wear regular clothes which are neat and clean
   C. try to wear a uniform or other disguise to help the investigation
   D. wear old clothes in poor neighborhoods and wear better clothes when inspecting better stores

10. Assume that during the course of inspection of a store you have found a violation of your regulations and told the store manager. He became angry and shoved you. You should

    A. call the police   B. leave immediately
    C. shove him back   D. try to calm him down

11. Suppose one of the large daily newspapers runs an exposé of the adulteration of meat by a big supermarket chain. This firm has a large store in the area to which you have been assigned. You notice that you are not scheduled to inspect this store for several weeks.
    The one of the following that you should do FIRST is to

    A. write to the newspaper in the name of the Division of Consumer Affairs asking where the reporters obtained their facts
    B. follow your normal schedule unless you are directed otherwise
    C. inspect the supermarket on your own time
    D. move back your other inspection assignments so that you can inspect the supermarket immediately

12. If you are going to investigate a retail store and the store manager refuses to talk to you, you should

    A. ask him what he is trying to hide
    B. call the police for help
    C. leave quietly and report the circumstances to your superior
    D. tell him he will be fined and imprisoned for non-cooperation

13. Assume that you are carrying out a routine inspection of a supermarket. During the inspection, the store manager approaches you and asks to see your identification badge. You should

    A. ask him why he wants to see your identification
    B. explain that you are not required to carry your identification badge with you
    C. insist that he show you his identification first
    D. show him your identification badge

14. Suppose that during the course of an inspection an Inspector discovers that a measuring device on the premises is not accurate. The one of the following that he should do FIRST is to

    A. confiscate the measuring device and remove it from the premises
    B. destroy the measuring device with the owner's permission
    C. give the owner an opportunity to repair the measuring device
    D. issue a violation for using defective equipment

15. Assume that you are making a routine inspection of a retail store when you notice in a display of electric broilers, a size and model which you have been looking for for several weeks but have been unable to find. Of the following, the BEST thing for you to do is to

    A. ask the store owner to put one of the broilers aside for you and come back to purchase it after working hours
    B. purchase the broiler at the store after you have completed your inspection there
    C. say nothing about the broiler to the store owner and purchase the broiler at a store outside your inspection territory
    D. tell the store owner that you would really like to have a broiler like that one

16. The following foods contain standardized ingredients EXCEPT

    A. ice cream   B. jams and jellies
    C. ketchup   D. orange drink

17. Earthenware dishes very often affect food stored in them by being the source of 17.___

    A. asbestos contamination
    B. bacteria
    C. lead contamination
    D. fluid dyes

18. The presence of E. Coli in food PROBABLY means that it 18.___

    A. is contaminated by fecal matter
    B. is high in minerals
    C. is suitable for diabetics
    D. must be refrigerated

19. Of the following procedures, the one which generally occurs directly before an Inspector is notified to appear at a hearing regarding a violation is the 19.___

    A. placing of the complaint on the hearings calendar
    B. preparation of the complaint in an area office
    C. submission of the complaint and supporting affidavits to the proper departmental official
    D. swearing to the complaint by the Inspector

20. Assume that you are testifying at a hearing for a violation you issued. You are asked a question, but before you are able to answer it, the attorney for the defendant raises an objection. You should 20.___

    A. answer the question as truthfully as you can
    B. refuse to answer the question until you have consulted with the attorney for the Department
    C. say nothing until the hearing officer rules on the objection
    D. tell the hearing officer that you do not know the answer to the question

21. To prepare for testimony in court concerning a violation of the Regulations, the Inspector should 21.___

    A. go over the notes he took at the time of the violation and have them ready in court to refresh his memory
    B. memorize all the details of the case
    C. read books on criminal law
    D. wear his best clothes to court

22. The purpose of calling a Board of Review when a defendant pleads *not guilty* to a violation of regulations of the Department is to 22.___

    A. consider the relevant facts and evidence and how they relate to the statute in question
    B. determine whether the statute in question has loopholes which must be eliminated
    C. provide administrative personnel of the Department with an opportunity to reassess the complaint procedure
    D. re-examine the procedures followed by the complaining Inspector to determine whether he acted correctly

23. When an Inspector issues a summons to a corporation, the one of the following that he MUST do is to

   A. inform the main office in a written memorandum that a summons has been issued to a corporate firm
   B. obtain certification of the corporation's existence from the federal government
   C. submit a statement signed by the corporation president supplying the date of incorporation
   D. submit data necessary to get written certification of the corporation's existence

24. Assume that you are about to enter the meat packaging room of a supermarket to inspect the scales when you see that someone has spilled a large quantity of water on the floor. It would be BEST for you to

   A. ask the store manager to lend you a pair of boots to protect your shoes while you make the inspection
   B. ask the store manager to mop up the water so you don't slip on it
   C. make the inspection, since water on the floor will not affect the results
   D. refuse to make the inspection because of the unclean conditions in the store

25. Assume that you have a bad cold and take a strong decongestant pill before you come to work. You are scheduled that day to drive an official car to a supermarket to make an inspection. Of the following, it would be BEST for you to

   A. drive to the store and make the inspection as usual
   B. drive to the store very slowly and carefully, since you are not feeling well
   C. explain to your supervisor that you should not drive that day
   D. start out to make the inspection, but return to the office if you feel your driving ability is impaired

26. Assume that you cut your hand slightly while working in your office. Of the following, the BEST thing for you to do would be to

   A. clean the cut when you get home that evening
   B. fill out an accident report
   C. notify your supervisor
   D. wash the cut and put a bandaid on it

27. Of the following office supplies, the kind which you should usually be MOST careful to keep away from an open flame is

   A. carbon paper   B. ink
   C. paste   D. typing paper

28. The only one of the following types of fire extinguishers which should generally NOT be used to extinguish a gasoline fire is

   A. carbon dioxide   B. dry chemical
   C. foam   D. water

Questions 29-32.

   DIRECTIONS: Questions 29 through 32 are to be answered SOLELY on the information contained in the chart below.

COMPARATIVE WEIGHTS AND PRICES FOR 4 BRANDS OF PARMESAN CHEESE

PRICES	SMALL	MEDIUM	LARGE	EXTRA LARGE
Brand W	29¢	63¢	$1.30	$1.84
Brand X	18¢	48¢	.90	1.35
Brand Y	30¢	55¢	1.43	1.92
Brand Z	15¢	29¢	.84	1.56

WEIGHTS (IN OUNCES)	SMALL	MEDIUM	LARGE	EXTRA LARGE
Brand W	2	4 1/2	10	16
Brand X	1 1/2	4	9	15
Brand Y	2 1/2	5 1/2	11	16
Brand Z	1	2	6	12

29. Of the following, the brand and size of cheese which costs LEAST per ounce is Brand 29._____

    A. W, large   B. X, extra large
    C. Y, medium   D. Z, extra large

30. The brand which comes in a small size that costs the same per ounce as the extra large 30._____
size is brand

    A. W   B. X   C. Y   D. Z

31. Using a combination of the sizes listed in the above chart, the LEAST expensive price for 31._____
exactly 1 pound, 11 ounces of Brand Z would be

    A. $3.13   B. $3.56   C. $3.70   D. $4.68

32. In the medium size, the brand that is LEAST expensive per ounce is Brand 32._____

    A. W   B. X   C. Y   D. Z

Questions 33-35.

DIRECTIONS: Questions 33 through 35 are to be answered SOLELY on the information contained in the charts on the following page.

EDUCATIONAL LEVEL ATTAINED BY HIGH SCHOOL STUDENTS ENTERING HIGH SCHOOL IN 1968 AND 2018

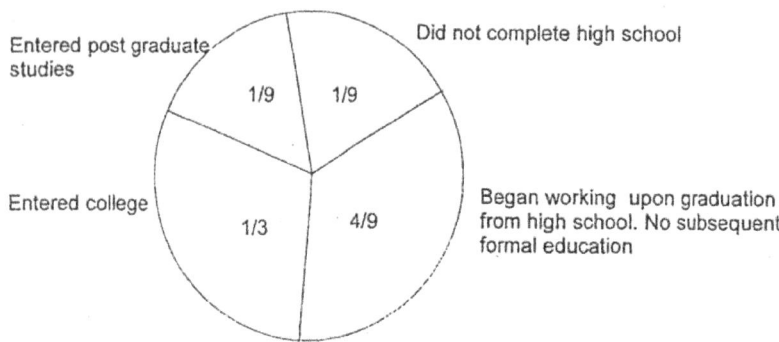

ENTERING CLASS OF 1968 – TOTAL OF 117

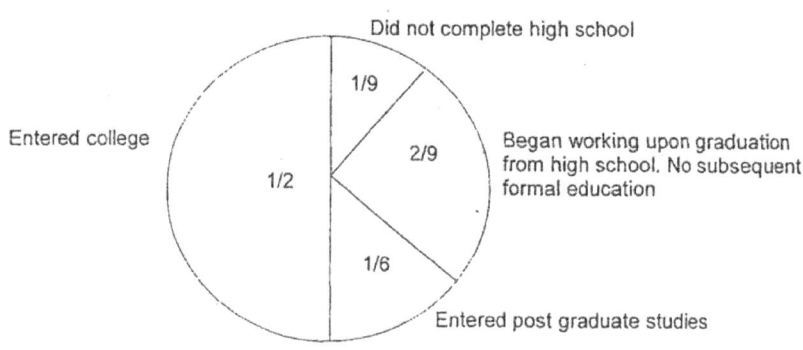

ENTERING CLASS OF 2018 – TOTAL OF 180

33. The total number of students from both classes who went to work immediately after high school graduation was

    A. 33   B. 40   C. 92   D. 129

34. Assuming that half of the students who did not complete high school received equivalency diplomas which gives them the status of high school graduates, the total number of 2018 high school freshmen who eventually achieved the level of high school graduation was

    A. 50   B. 130   C. 150   D. 170

35. What was the approximate percentage increase in the students entering college (including those entering post-graduate studies) between the classes entering in, 1968 and 2018?

    A. 6%   B. 15%   C. 22%   D. 45%

KEY (CORRECT ANSWERS)

1.	C	16.	D
2.	C	17.	C
3.	C	18.	A
4.	B	19.	A
5.	D	20.	C
6.	A	21.	A
7.	D	22.	A
8.	A	23.	D
9.	B	24.	B
10.	D	25.	C
11.	B	26.	D
12.	C	27.	A
13.	D	28.	D
14.	C	29.	B
15.	C	30.	C

31. B
32. C
33. C
34. D
35. C

EXAMINATION SECTION
TEST 1

DIRECTIONS: Each question or incomplete statement is followed by several suggested answers or completions. Select the one that BEST answers the question or completes the statement. *PRINT THE LETTER OF THE CORRECT ANSWER IN THE SPACE AT THE RIGHT.*

1. The one of the following which is the BEST description of a properly objective investigator is one who

    A. is friendly and sensitive to the client's feelings, without becoming emotionally involved
    B. is distant and impersonal, remaining unaffected by what the client says
    C. lets personal emotions enter as far as the client's situation calls for them
    D. becomes emotionally involved with the client's situation but without showing this involvement

    1.____

2. The one of the following which is MOST necessary for successfully interviewing a person who belongs to a culture different from that of the investigator is for the investigator to

    A. have some appreciation of the other culture
    B. ignore those cultural differences which lead to bias
    C. stay away from sensitive, "touchy" issues
    D. assume the mannerisms of people in the other cultures

    2.____

3. In fact-finding interviews, it is generally assumed that the smaller the number of interviewees, the greater the increase of reliability with the addition of others. The PROPER number of interviewees needed to insure the accuracy of information obtained *generally* depends upon the

    A. educational level of those interviewed
    B. number of people who have the required information
    C. directness of the questions asked
    D. variability of the information received

    3.____

4. The one of the following which is generally MOST likely to be accurately described in an interview by an interviewee is

    A. the presence of a large painting in the investigator's office
    B. the number of people in the investigator's waiting room
    C. space relations
    D. duration of time

    4.____

5. The one of the following which is *generally* the BEST course of action for an investigator to take when interviewing a person who is reluctant to tell what he knows about a matter under investigation is to

    A. be curt and abrupt and threaten the person with the consequences of his withholding information
    B. be firm and severe and pressure the person into telling the needed information
    C. be patient and candid with the person being questioned about the investigation since doing otherwise is not ethical

    5.____

D. give the person false information about the investigation so he will give the needed information without realizing its importance

6. It is often recommended that an investigator prepare in advance a list of questions or topics to be covered in an interview. The MAIN reason for using such a check list is to

   A. allow investigations to be assigned to less efficient investigators
   B. eliminate a large amount of follow-up paper work
   C. aid the investigator in remembering to cover all important topics
   D. aid the investigator in maintaining an objective distance from the person interviewed

7. Usually, the CHIEF advantage of a directive approach in an interview is that

   A. the investigator maintains control over the course of the interview
   B. the person interviewed is more likely to be put at ease
   C. the person interviewed is generally left free to direct the interview
   D. the investigator will not suggest answers to the person interviewed

8. Usually, the CHIEF advantage of a non-directive approach by an investigator in conducting an interview is that

   A. the investigator generally conceals what he is looking for in the interview
   B. the person interviewed is more likely to express his true feelings about the topic under discussion
   C. the person interviewed is more likely to follow an idea introduced by the investigator
   D. the investigator can keep the discussion limited to topics he believes to be relevant

9. The one of the following which is generally the *least likely* to be accurate in a description of an event given to an investigator is a statement about

   A. the presence of an object
   B. the number of people, when their number is small
   C. locations of people
   D. duration of time

10. Assume that you, an investigator, are conducting a character investigation. In an interview, the one of the following character traits of the person being interviewed which can USUALLY be determined with a *good* degree of reliability is

    A. honesty
    B. dependability
    C. forcefulness
    D. perseverance

11. As an investigator, you have been assigned the task of obtaining a family's social history. The BEST place for you to interview members of the family while obtaining this social history would *generally* be in

    A. the family's home
    B. your agency's general offices
    C. the home of a friend of the family
    D. your own private office

12. You, an investigator, are checking someone's work history. The way for you to get the MOST reliable information from a previous employer is to

    A. send personal letters; the employer will respond to the personal attention
    B. send form letters; the employer will cooperate readily since little time or effort is asked of him
    C. arrange a personal interview; the employer may offer information he would not care to put in a letter or speak over the phone
    D. telephone; this method is as effective as a personal interview and is much more convenient

13. The effect that attestation, or the formal taking of an oath, has on witness testimony is to

    A. decrease accuracy, since a witness under oath is more nervous about what is said
    B. make little difference, since the witness is not too swayed by an oath
    C. increase accuracy, since a witness under oath feels more responsibility for what is said
    D. eliminate inaccuracy unless there is deliberate perjury on the part of the witness

14. If an investigator obtains testimony from persons in interviews by means of interrogation or asking questions rather than by letting the person freely relate the testimony, what is said will GENERALLY be

    A. greater in range and less accurate
    B. greater in range and more accurate
    C. about the same in range and less accurate
    D. about the same in range and more accurate

15. Experienced investigators have learned to phrase their questions carefully in order to obtain the desired response. Of the following, the question which would *usually* elicit the MOST accurate answer is:

    A. "How old are you?"
    B. "What is your income?"
    C. "How are you today?"
    D. "What is the date of your birth?"

16. The one of the following questions which would *generally* lead to the LEAST reliable answer is

    A. "Did you see a wallet?"
    B. "Was the German Shepherd gray?"
    C. "Didn't you see the stop sign?"
    D. "Did you see the guard on duty?"

17. Some investigators may make a practice of observing details of the surroundings when interviewing in someone's home or office. Such a practice is *generally* considered

    A. *undesirable,* mainly because such snooping is an unwarranted, unethical invasion of privacy
    B. *undesirable,* mainly because useful information is rarely, if ever, gained this way
    C. *desirable,* mainly because, useful insights into the character of the person interviewed may be gained

D. *desirable,* mainly because it is impossible to evaluate a person adequately without such observation of his environment

18. The one of the following questions which will MOST often lead to a reliable answer is: 18.____

    A. "Was his hair very dark?"
    B. "Wasn't there a clock on the wall?"
    C. "Was the automobile white or gray?"
    D. "Did you see a motorcycle?"

19. The one of the following which can MOST accurately be determined by an investigator by means of interviewing is 19.____

    A. a persons's intelligence
    B. factual information about an event
    C. a person's aptitude for a specific task
    D. a person's perceptions of his own abilities

20. The one of the following which is *most likely* to help a person being interviewed feel at ease is for the investigator to 20.____

    A. let him start the conversation
    B. give him an abundance of time
    C. be relaxed himself
    D. open the interview by telling a joke

21. If the interviewee is to perceive some goal for himself in the interview and thus be motivated to participate in it, it is important that he clearly understand some of the aspects of the interview. Of the following aspects, the one the interviewee needs LEAST to understand is 21.____

    A. the purpose of the interview
    B. the mechanics of interviewing
    C. the use made of the information he contributes
    D. what will be expected of him in the interview

22. As an investigator working on a project requiring inter-agency cooperation, you find that employees of an agency involved in the project are constantly making it difficult for you to obtain necessary information. Of the following, the BEST action for you to take FIRST is to 22.____

    A. discuss the problem with your supervisor
    B. speak with your counterpart in the other agency
    C. discuss the problem with the head of the uncooperative agency
    D. contact the head of your agency

23. The investigator is justified in misleading the interviewee only when, in the investigator's judgment, this is clearly required by the problem being investigated. Such practice is 23.____

    A. *necessary;* there are times when complete honesty will impede a successful investigation
    B. *unnecessary ;* such a tactic is unethical and should never be employed
    C. *necessary;* an investigator must be guided by success rather than ethical considerations in an investigation

D. *unnecessary;* it is clearly doubtful whether such a practice will help the investigator conclude the investigation successfully

24. Assume that, in investigating a case of possible welfare fraud, it becomes necessary to hold an interview in the client's home in order to observe family interaction and conditions. Upon arriving, the investigator finds that the client's living room is noisy and crowded, with neighbors present and children running in and out. Of the following, the BEST course of action for the investigator to take is to

    A. conduct the interview in the living room after telling the children to behave, and asking the neighbors to leave
    B. tell the client that it is impossible to conduct the interview in the apartment, and make an appointment for the next day in the investigator's office
    C. suggest that they move from the living room into the kitchen where there is a table on which he can write
    D. try his best to conduct the interview in the noisy and crowded living room

25. You, an investigator, are giving testimony in court about a matter you have investigated. An attorney is questioning you in an abrasive, badgering way, and, in an insulting manner, calls into doubt your ability as an investigator. You lose your temper and respond angrily, telling the attorney to stop harassing and insulting you. Of the following, the BEST description of such a response is that it is *generally*

    A. *appropriate;* as a witness in court, you do not have to take insults from anybody, including an attorney
    B. *inappropriate; losing your* temper will show that you are weak and cannot be trusted as an investigator
    C. *appropriate;* a judge and jury will usually respect someone who responds strongly to unjust provocation
    D. *inappropriate;* such conduct is unprofessional and may unfavorably impress a judge and jury

KEY (CORRECT ANSWERS)

1.	A	11.	A
2.	A	12.	C
3.	D	13.	C
4.	A	14.	A
5.	C	15.	D
6.	C	16.	B
7.	A	17.	C
8.	B	18.	D
9.	D	19.	D
10.	C	20.	C

21. B
22. A
23. A
24. C
25. D

TEST 2

DIRECTIONS: Each question or incomplete statement is followed by several suggested answers or completions. Select the one that BEST answers the question or completes the statement. *PRINT THE LETTER OF THE CORRECT ANSWER IN THE SPACE AT THE RIGHT.*

1. The reliability of information obtained increases with the number of persons interviewed. The more the interviewees differ in their statements, the more persons it is necessary to interview to ascertain the true facts. According to this statement, the dependability of the information about an occurrence obtained from interviews is related to

    A. how many people are interviewed
    B. how soon after the occurrence an interview can be arranged
    C. the individual technique of the interviewer
    D. the interviewer's ability to detect differences in the statements of interviewees

    1.____

2. An investigator interviews members of the public at his desk. The attitude of the public toward this department will probably be LEAST affected by this investigator's

    A. courtesy	B. efficiency
    C. height	D. neatness

    2.____

3. The *one* of the following which is NOT effective in obtaining complete testimony from a witness during an interview is to

    A. ask questions in chronological order
    B. permit the witness to structure the interview
    C. make sure you fully understand the response to each question
    D. review questions to be asked beforehand

    3.____

4. The person MOST likely to be a good interviewer is one who

    A. is able to outguess the person being interviewed
    B. tries to change the attitudes of the persons he interviews
    C. controls the interview by skillfully dominating the conversation
    D. is able to imagine himself in the position of the person being interviewed

    4.____

5. When you are interviewing someone to obtain information, the BEST of the following reasons for you to repeat certain of his exact words is to

    A. *assure* him that appropriate action will be taken
    B. *encourage* him to elaborate on a point he has made
    C. *assure* him that you agree with his point of view
    D. *encourage* him to switch to another topic of discussion

    5.____

6. You are interviewing a client who has just been assaulted. He has trouble collecting his thoughts and telling his story coherently. Which of the following represents the MOST effective method of questioning under these circumstances?

    A. Ask questions which structure the client's story chronologically into units, each with a beginning, middle and end.
    B. Ask several questions at a time to structure the interview.

    6.____

C. Ask open-ended questions which allow the client to respond in a variety of ways.
D. Begin the interview with several detailed questions in order to focus the client's attention on the situation.

7. You are conducting an initial interview with a witness who expresses reluctance, even hostility, to being questioned. You feel it would be helpful to take some notes during the interview.
In this situation, it would be BEST to

   A. put off note-taking until a follow-up interview, and concentrate on establishing rapport with the witness
   B. explain the necessity of note-taking, and proceed to take notes during the interview
   C. make notes from memory after the witness has left
   D. take notes, but as unobtrusively as possible

7.____

8. You are interviewing the owner of a stolen car about facts relating to the robbery. After completing his statement, the car owner suddenly states that some of the details he has just related are not correct. You realize that this change might be significant.
Of the following, it would be BEST for you to

   A. ask the owner what other details he may have given incorrectly
   B. make a note of the discrepancy for discussion at a later date
   C. repeat your questioning on the details that were misstated until you have covered that area completely
   D. explain to the owner that because of his change of testimony, you will have to repeat the entire interview

8.____

9. Assume that you have been asked to get all the pertinent information from an employee who claims that she witnessed a robbery.
Which of the following questions is *least likely* to influence the witness's response?

   A. "Can you describe the robber's hair?"
   B. "Did the robber have a lot of hair?"
   C. "Was the robber's hair black or brown?"
   D. "Was the robber's hair very dark?"

9.____

10. In order to obtain an accurate statement from a person who has witnessed a crime, it is BEST to question the witness

    A. as soon as possible after the crime was committed
    B. after the witness has discussed the crime with other witnesses
    C. after the witness has had sufficient time to reflect on events and formulate a logical statement
    D. after the witness has been advised that he is obligated to tell the whole truth

10.____

11. Assume that your superior assigns you to interview an individual who, he warns, seems to be hightly "introverted." You should be aware that, during an interview, such a person is likely to

    A. hold views which are highly controversial in nature
    B. be domineering and try to control the direction of the interview
    C. resist answering personal questions regarding his background
    D. give information which is largely fabricated

11.____

12. A young woman was stabbed in the hand in her home by her estranged boyfriend. Her mother and two sisters were at home at the time.
    Of the following, it would generally be BEST to interview the young woman in the presence of

    A. her mother *only*
    B. all members of her immediate family
    C. members of the family who actually observed the crime
    D. the official authorities

13. The one of the following statements concerning interviewing which is LEAST valid is that

    A. skill in interviewing can be improved by knowledge of the basic factors involving relations between people
    B. interviewing should become a routine and mechanical practice to the skilled and experienced interviewer
    C. genuine interest in people is essential for successful interviewing
    D. certain psychological traits characterize most people most of the time

14. The initial interview will normally be more of a problem to the interviewer than any subsequent interviews he may have with the same person because

    A. the interviewee is likely to be hostile
    B. there is too much to be accomplished in one session
    C. he has less information about the client than he will have later
    D. some information may be forgotten when later making record of this first interview

15. Continuous taking of notes during an interview is generally

    A. *desirable* because no important facts will be forgotten
    B. *undesirable* because it gives the person being interviewed a clue to the importance of the information being obtained from him
    C. *desirable* because the interviewer cannot write as fast as the person being interviewed can speak
    D. *undesirable* because it may put the person being interviewed ill at ease

16. "Carefully planned interviews tend to impose restrictions which leave little room for spontaneity." A flaw in this critiscism of the planned interview is that it does NOT take into account that

    A. a planned interview obviates the need for spontaneity
    B. even the planned interview may be flexible
    C. not all planned interviews impose restrictions
    D. restrictions that result from planning are undesirable

17. Writing up the interview into a systematic report is BEST done

    A. in the presence of the subject, so that mistakes can be corrected immediately
    B. within a reasonably short time after the interview, so that nothing is forgotten
    C. no sooner than several days after the interview, so that the interviewer will have had plenty of time to think about it
    D. with the help of someone not present at the interview, so that an objective view can be obtained

18. While you are conducting an interview, the telephone on your desk rings. Of the following, it would be BEST for you to

    A. ask the interviewer at the next desk to answer your telephone and take the message for you
    B. excuse yourself, pick up the telephone, and tell the person on the other end you are busy and will call him back later
    C. ignore the ringing telephone and continue with the interview
    D. use another telephone to inform the operator not to put calls through to you while you are conducting an interview

19. An interviewee is at your desk, which is quite near to desks where other people work. He beckons you a little closer and starts to talk in a low voice as though he does not want anyone else to hear him. Under these circumstances, the BEST thing for you to do is to

    A. ask him to speak a little louder so that he can be heard
    B. cut the interview short and not get involved in his problems
    C. explain that people at other desks are not eavesdroppers
    D. listen carefully to what he says and give it consideration

20. Of the following, the BEST way for a person to develop competence as an interviewer is to

    A. attend lectures on interviewing techniques
    B. practice with employees on the job
    C. conduct interviews under the supervision of an experienced instructor
    D. attend a training course in counseling

21. During the course of an interview, it would be LEAST desirable for the investigator to

    A. correct immediately any grammatical errors made by an interviewee
    B. express himself in such a way as to be clearly understood
    C. restrict the interviewee to the subject of the interview
    D. make notes in a way that will not disturb the interviewee

22. Suppose that you are interviewing an eleven year old boy. The CHIEF point among the following for you to keep in mind is that a child, as compared with an adult, is generally

    A. more likely to attempt to conceal information
    B. a person of lower intelligence
    C. more garrulous
    D. more receptive to suggestive questions

23. In interviewing a person, "suggestive questions" should be avoided because, among the following,

    A. the answers to leading questions are not admissible in evidence
    B. an investigator must be fair and impartial
    C. the interrogation of a witness must be formulated according to his mentality
    D. they are less apt to lead to the truth

24. Among the following, it is generally desirable to interview a person outside his home or office because

A. the presence of relatives and friends may prevent him from speaking freely
B. a person's surroundings tend to color his testimony
C. the person will find less distraction outside his home or office
D. a person tends to dominate the interview when in familiar surroundings

25. For the interviewing process to be MOST successful, the interviewer should generally 25._____

   A. remind the person being interviewed that false statements will constitute perjury and will be prosecuted as such
   B. devise a single and unvarying pattern for all interviewing situations
   C. let the individual being interviewed control the content of the interview but not its length
   D. vary his interviewing approach as the situation requires it

KEY (CORRECT ANSWERS)

1.	A	11.	C
2.	C	12.	D
3.	B	13.	B
4.	D	14.	C
5.	B	15.	D
6.	A	16.	B
7.	B	17.	B
8.	C	18.	B
9.	A	19.	D
10.	A	20.	C

21.	A
22.	D
23.	D
24.	A
25.	D

EXAMINATION SECTION
TEST 1

DIRECTIONS: Each question or incomplete statement is followed by several suggested answers or completions. Select the one that BEST answers the question or completes the statement. *PRINT THE LETTER OF THE CORRECT ANSWER IN THE SPACE AT THE RIGHT.*

1. Which of the following is the BEST way to get an accurate account of an incident?

    A. Interview those involved immediately
    B. Interview those involved as soon as possible
    C. Wait until you review the official reports and then interview those involved as soon as possible
    D. Carefully observe a videotaped simulation

2. While conducting investigations, it is necessary to pay close attention to nonverbal communication.
   This would include all of the following EXCEPT

    A. analyzing each individual's behavior as it arises
    B. paying attention to the person's tone of voice
    C. viewing the nonverbal messages as indicators
    D. noting discrepancies between verbal and nonverbal messages

3. While conducting an interview, it is MOST important to

    A. ignore your own values and past experiences
    B. utilize your own values and past experiences in recording information
    C. explain your own values to those you are interviewing
    D. be aware of your own values and experiences and of how they might influence the interview

4. Of the following, which is the BEST way to question a witness?

    A. Ask pointed questions
    B. Talk in a clipped manner
    C. Talk aimlessly
    D. Ask random questions

5. You are interviewing an uncooperative person.
   Of the following, the FIRST thing you should do in this situation is to

    A. try various appeals to win the person over to a cooperative attitude
    B. try to ascertain the reason for noncooperation
    C. promise the person that all data will be kept confidential
    D. alter the interviewing technique

6. Which of the following is the BEST way to make a witness feel at ease?

    A. Reassure him or her of the importance of the situation
    B. Tell the witness that any comments he or she makes will be of no use if the witness is too nervous

C. Allow the witness a little extra time to collect his or her thoughts
D. Maintain a friendly attitude

7. Which of the following behaviors would be the WORST to display during an investigative interview?   7._____

   A. Being unfocused
   B. Displaying uncertainty about some departmental regulations
   C. Acting biased
   D. Acting like you are overloaded with work

8. Investigations should be conducted with all of the following EXCEPT   8._____

   A. objectivity   B. speed
   C. subjectivity   D. thoroughness

9. When trying to help someone focus during an interview, it is BEST to   9._____

   A. use an open-ended question
   B. offer to reschedule at a time when the person is better prepared
   C. ask the person being interviewed to summarize the situation
   D. use a close-ended question

10. There are usually four stages during an interview: preparation, opening, conducting, and closing.   10._____
    All of the following are steps included in the closing stage of an interview EXCEPT

    A. verifying information
    B. stating the continuing responsibilities, if any, of the person being interviewed
    C. summarizing
    D. describing any additional steps that may need to be taken

11. During an employment interview, which of the following questions can legally be asked?   11._____

    A. What is your nationality?
    B. Are you at least 18 years of age?
    C. Do you wish to be addressed as Miss, Mrs., or Ms.?
    D. Do you have a disability?

12. As you continue talking with a man you are interviewing, you have the feeling that some of his answers to earlier questions were not totally correct. You think that he might have been afraid or confused earlier, but that the interview has now put him in a more comfortable frame of mind.   12._____
    In order to test the reliability of information received from the earlier questions, the BEST thing for you to do now is to ask new questions that

    A. allow him to explain why he deliberately gave you false information
    B. would yield the same information but are worded differently
    C. put pressure on him so that he personally wants to clear up the facts in his earlier answers
    D. indicate to him that you are aware of his deceptive-ness

13. When investigating a situation, it is MOST important that those whom you have questioned

    A. feel that you are unbiased
    B. feel comfortable around you
    C. feel confident in your abilities
    D. admire your investigative skills

14. All of the following are examples of flight defenses EXCEPT

    A. rationalization
    B. talking about problems excessively
    C. using threatening language
    D. withdrawing

15. Assume that you have been assigned to conduct a follow-up interview with a primary witness whom you would like to have testify at an important hearing.
    Under these circumstances, it is MOST important to

    A. do your best to ensure that the witness remains cooperative
    B. conduct the matter in secret
    C. allow the witness to determine where and when the interview takes place
    D. conduct the interview as soon as possible to ensure a strong case

16. You are interviewing someone who is under a great deal of stress. He is talking continuously and rambling, making it difficult for you to obtain the information you need.
    In order to make the interview more successful, it would be BEST for you to

    A. interrupt him and ask him specific questions in order to get the information you need
    B. tell him that his rambling is causing you a lot of problems
    C. let him continue talking for as long as he wishes
    D. ask him to get to the point because you need to interview others

17. When an investigator first arrives at the scene of an incident, it is MOST important for him or her to be sure that

    A. all of the witnesses are telling the truth
    B. no additional physical evidence is destroyed
    C. all of the witnesses agree with each other about what they observed
    D. the witnesses do not become angry

18. All of the following statements about nonverbal communication are true EXCEPT:

    A. Nonverbal communication is easily controlled
    B. Much of the meaning of a message is transmitted through nonverbal behavior
    C. Nonverbal behaviors can reveal hidden agendas
    D. Nonverbal signals can help the interviewer determine if the person being interviewed is confused but unwilling to admit it

4 (#1)

19. For state agencies, a properly conducted investigation might do any of the following EXCEPT

   A. discover the cause of a workplace accident
   B. uncover tax fraud or unfair labor practices by an employer
   C. provide a supervisor with effective supervisory methods
   D. uncover information critical to determining the outcome of an employee grievance

20. In interviewing, the practice of verbally anticipating the other person's answers to your questions is generally

   A. *desirable*, because it is effective and economical when interviewing large numbers of people
   B. *desirable*, because many people have language difficulties
   C. *undesirable*, because it is the right of every person to answer however he or she wishes
   D. *undesirable*, because the person being interviewed may be led to agree with the answer proposed by the interviewer even when the answer is not entirely correct

KEY (CORRECT ANSWERS)

1. A	6. D	11. B	16. A
2. A	7. C	12. B	17. B
3. D	8. C	13. A	18. A
4. A	9. D	14. C	19. C
5. B	10. A	15. A	20. D

TEST 2

DIRECTIONS: Each question or incomplete statement is followed by several suggested answers or completions. Select the one that BEST answers the question or completes the statement. *PRINT THE LETTER OF THE CORRECT ANSWER IN THE SPACE AT THE RIGHT.*

1. All of the following are good examples of the volatile and vulnerable nature of evidence EXCEPT

    A. those involved may be intimidated to forget or to make up key elements of testimony
    B. physical evidence can disappear
    C. two extra copies are made of a valuable floppy disk
    D. water that caused an industrial accident can dry up

2. You find that many of the people you interview are verbally abusive and unusually hostile to you.
Of the following, the MOST appropriate action for you to take FIRST is to

    A. review your interviewing techniques and consider whether you may be somehow provoking those you interview
    B. act in a more authoritative manner when interviewing troublesome interviewees
    C. tell those people that you will not be able to help them unless their troublesome behavior ceases
    D. disregard the troublesome behavior and proceed as you would normally

3. Of the following statements, which is the MOST accurate?

    A. Good investigative techniques are easily learned.
    B. Witnesses should be given a lot of time to collect their thoughts before being interviewed.
    C. The more standardized and thought out the investigative procedures, the better the chance that the investigation will be successful.
    D. Statements taken from witnesses are not usually a critical to an investigation and subsequent action as some experts claim.

4. The information sought in an interview is sometimes fixed in advance by a printed form or specific instructions from an interviewer's supervisor.
Because of this, it is IMPORTANT to

    A. use your own judgment as to whether or not these questions should be used in the interview
    B. have the form in front of you so you can read from it and not miss any important points when interviewing
    C. make a copy of the form and give it to the client to complete
    D. be thoroughly acquainted with the purpose behind each question and understand its significance

5. As an investigator, you perform field work in order to enforce state labor laws.
If no set agency policy is in effect, it would MOST likely be the highest priority to investigate a report of

A. a minimum wage violation
B. nonpayment of overtime wages to an employee
C. nonpayment to a worker in an industrial homework setting
D. systematic nonpayment to farm workers

6. In order to get the maximum amount of information from someone during an interview, it is MOST important for the interviewer to communicate to the person being interviewed the feeling that the interviewer is

    A. interested in what the person has to say
    B. a figure of authority
    C. efficient in his or her work habits
    D. sympathetic to the lifestyle of the person being interviewed

7. When an initial interview is being conducted, one way of starting is to explain the purpose of the interview to the person being interviewed.
The practice of starting the interview with such an explanation is GENERALLY

    A. *desirable,* because the person can then understand why the interview is necessary and what it should accomplish
    B. *desirable,* because it creates the rapport which is necessary to successful interviewing
    C. *undesirable,* because time will be saved if starting off directly with the questions which must be asked
    D. *undesirable,* because the interviewer should have the choice of starting an interview in the manner that he or she prefers

8. The GREATEST problem for investigators is when witnesses

    A. are so eager to cooperate that they frequently interrupt the investigator
    B. become a little bored telling and retelling what they have observed
    C. are not very willing to cooperate
    D. are eager to get back to work

9. Two important skills sometimes used during an interview are giving behavioral feedback and confronting.
What is the key difference between the two?

    A. There is none; they are actually two different names for the same process.
    B. Confronting is threatening, but giving behavioral feedback is not.
    C. Behavioral feedback merely describes action, while confronting evaluates the consequences of behavior.
    D. Behavioral feedback requires equipment in order to test the response of the client.

10. If applied properly, *being a good listener* is a desirable interviewing technique PRIMARILY because it

    A. more easily catches the person being interviewed in misrepresentations and lies
    B. conserves the energies of the interviewer
    C. encourages the person being interviewed to talk about his or her personal affairs without restraint
    D. is more likely to secure information which is generally reliable and complete

11. A full-scale police criminal investigation

    A. should be avoided at all costs
    B. may be warranted in some cases
    C. most likely means the agency investigator did not do his or her job properly
    D. is not necessary in state agencies

12. Which of the following are usually the MOST effective techniques for handling difficult behaviors during an interview?
    I. Focusing on nondefensive behaviors
    II. Respecting silence; letting yourself and the person
    III. you are interviewing get emotions under control
    IV. Giving advice
    V. Avoiding upsetting issues

    The CORRECT answer is:

    A. II, III   B. I, II   C. III, IV   D. I, III, IV

13. Assume that you are conducting safety and health inspections in a wide variety of settings. The supervisor at one of the sites you must periodically inspect seems very anxious during your visits and always wants you to pinpoint exactly when you will be returning for your next inspection.
    It would be BEST to

    A. assume the supervisor has something to hide, so you will double the number of inspections at the site
    B. assume nothing
    C. assume the supervisor is just slightly neurotic
    D. check to see if the supervisor has a criminal record

14. Of the following, the MOST important characteristic for an interviewer to have is

    A. personal attractiveness   B. sincerity
    C. appealing personality   D. a sense of humor

15. It is MOST likely that the longer the time before statements are taken from witnesses, the more

    A. time the witnesses will have to accurately reflect on what has occurred
    B. likely it is that the witnesses will be totally unwilling to cooperate
    C. likely it is that some distortion will occur
    D. likely it is that the witnesses will be willing to cooperate

16. The person you are interviewing is making, what you feel are, distasteful remarks.
    Of the following, the BEST approach would be to

    A. selectively ignore the remarks
    B. question the person about the remarks
    C. confront the person
    D. ask the person to stop or ask him or her to leave the interview

17. Which of the following behaviors should concern investigators the MOST?

   A. The tendency of eyewitnesses to *homogenize* what they have seen when exchanging information or chatting about the incident
   B. Eyewitnesses who are clear about minor details
   C. Eyewitnesses who are a little nervous
   D. Eyewitnesses who dislike their supervisors intensely

18. Part of your job requires the investigation of possible state sales tax fraud by organizations.
    Which of the following would MOST likely trigger a full-scale investigation?

   A. An anonymous phone call involving possible large-scale sales tax fraud by an organization
   B. A salesclerk forgets to add the sales tax to your order
   C. A new business does not have their sales tax *Certificate of Authority* prominently displayed so customers can see it
   D. The books and receipts of a large organization show that sales tax was not collected on $75 worth of merchandise

19. All of the following are inquiries that cannot be legally asked during an employment interview EXCEPT:

   A. Where were you born?
   B. Are you planning on having children?
   C. Are you able to carry out all necessary job assignments and perform them in a safe manner?
   D. In case of an emergency or accident, what is the name and address of the person to be notified?

20. When investigating a situation, you are careful when asking questions to never indicate how you think the question should be answered.
    This practice is a good idea PRIMARILY because

   A. it shows those you interview that you have confidence in their intelligence
   B. you will be more likely to get truthful answers
   C. you will not be significantly influencing the answers of those you have interviewed
   D. you will impress them with your interviewing skills

KEY (CORRECT ANSWERS)

1. C	6. A	11. B	16. A
2. A	7. A	12. B	17. A
3. C	8. C	13. B	18. A
4. D	9. C	14. B	19. C
5. D	10. D	15. C	20. C

EXAMINATION SECTION
TEST 1

DIRECTIONS: Each question or incomplete statement is followed by several suggested answers or completions. Select the one that BEST answers the question or completes the statement. *PRINT THE LETTER OF THE CORRECT ANSWER IN THE SPACE AT THE RIGHT.*

1. An investigator uses *Forms A, B,* and *C* in filling out his investigation reports. He uses *Form B* five times as often as *Form A*, and he uses *Form C* three times as often as *Form B*. If the total number of all forms used by the investigator in a month equals 735, how many times was *Form B* used?

    A. 150   B. 175   C. 205   D. 235

    1._____

2. Of all the investigators in one agency, 25% work in a particular building. Of these, 12% have desks on the 14th floor.
What percentage of the investigators work in this building but do NOT have desks on the 14th floor?

    A. 12%   B. 13%   C. 22%   D. 23%

    2._____

3. An investigator is given two reports to read. *Report P* is 160 pages long and takes the investigator 3 hours and 20 minutes to read.
If *Report S* is 254 pages long and the investigator reads it at the same rate as he reads *Report P*, how long will it take him to read *Report S*? _____ hours _____ minutes.

    A. 4; 15   B. 4; 50   C. 5; 10   D. 5; 30

    3._____

4. A team of 6 investigators was assigned to interview 234 people.
If half the investigators conduct twice as many interviews as the other half, and the slow group interviews 12 persons a day, how many days would it take to complete this assignment? _____ days.

    A. 4 1/2   B. 5   C. 6   D. 6 1/2

    4._____

5. The investigators in one agency conduct an average of 12 interviews an hour from 10 A.M. to 12 noon and from 1 P.M. to 5 P.M. daily. The director of this agency knows from past experience that 20% of those called in to be interviewed are unable to keep the appointments that were scheduled.
If the director wants his staff to be kept occupied with interviews for the entire time period that has been set aside for this function, how many appointments should be scheduled for each day?

    A. 86   B. 90   C. 96   D. 101

    5._____

6. An investigator has a 430 page report to read. The first day, he is able to read 20 pages. The second day, he reads 10 pages more than the first day, and the third day, he reads 15 pages more than the second day.
If, on the following days, he continues to read at the same rate he was reading on the third day, he will complete the report on the _____ day.

    A. 7th   B. 8th   C. 10th   D. 11th

    6._____

7. The 36 investigators in an agency are each required to submit 25 investigation reports a week. These reports are filled out on a certain form, and only one copy of the form is needed per report.
   Allowing 20% for waste, how many packages of 45 forms a piece should be ordered for each weekly period?

   A. 15   B. 20   C. 25   D. 30

8. During the fiscal year, an investigative unit received $260 for stationery and telephone expenditures. It spent 43% for stationery and 1/3 of the balance for telephone service. The amount of money that was left at the end of the fiscal year was MOST NEARLY

   A. $49   B. $50   C. $99   D. $109

Questions 9-10.

DIRECTIONS: Answer Questions 9 and 10 SOLELY on the data given below.

Number of days absent per worker (sickness)	1	2	3	4	5	6	7	8 or Over
Number of workers	96	45	16	3	1	0	1	0

Total Number of Workers: 500
Period Covered: Jan. 1, 2015 - Dec. 31, 2015

9. The TOTAL number of man days lost due to illness in 2015 was

   A. 137   B. 154   C. 162   D. 258

10. Of the 500 workers studied, the number who lost NO days due to sickness in 2015 was

    A. 230   B. 298   C. 338   D. 372

Questions 11-13.

DIRECTIONS: Answer Questions 11 to 13 SOLELY on the basis of the following paragraphs.

The rise of urban-industrial society has complicated the social arrangements needed to regulate contacts between people. As a consequence, there has been an unprecedented increase in the volume of laws and regulations designed to control individual conduct and to govern the relationship of the individual to others. In a century, there has been an eight-fold increase in the crimes for which one may be prosecuted.

For these offenses, the courts have the ultimate responsibility for redressing wrongs and convicting the guilty. The body of legal precepts gives the impression of an abstract and evenhanded dispensation of justice. Actually, the personnel of the agencies applying these precepts are faced with the difficulties of fitting abstract principles to highly variable situations emerging from the dynamics of everyday life. It is inevitable that discrepancies should exist between precept and practice.

The legal institutions serve as a framework for the social order by their slowness to respond to the caprices of transitory fad. This valuable contribution exacts a price in terms of the inflexibility of legal institutions in responding to new circumstances. This possibility is promoted by the changes in values and norms of the dynamic larger culture of which the legal precepts are a part.

11. According to the above passage, the increase in the number of laws and regulations during the twentieth century can be attributed to the

    A. complexity of modern industrial society
    B. increased seriousness of offenses committed
    C. growth of individualism
    D. anonymity of urban living

11.____

12. According to the above passage, which of the following presents a problem to the staff of legal agencies? The

    A. need to eliminate the discrepancy between precept and practice
    B. necessity to apply abstract legal precepts to rapidly changing conditions
    C. responsibility for reducing the number of abstract legal principles
    D. responsibility for understanding offenses in terms of the real-life situations from which they emerge

12.____

13. According to the above passage, it can be concluded that legal institutions affect social institutions by

    A. preventing change
    B. keeping pace with its norms and values
    C. changing its norms and values
    D. providing stability

13.____

Questions 14-16.

DIRECTIONS: Answer Questions 14 through 16 SOLELY on the basis of information given in the passage below.

A personnel interviewer, selecting job applicants, may find that he reacts badly to some people even on first contact. This reaction cannot usually be explained by things that the interviewee has done or said. Most of us have had the experience of liking or disliking, of feeling comfortable or uncomfortable with people on first acquaintance, long before we have had a chance to make a conscious, rational decision about them. Often, too, our liking or disliking is transmitted to the other person by subtle processes such as gestures, posture, voice intonations, or choice of words. The point to be kept in mind is this: the relations between people are complex and occur at several levels, from the conscious to the unconscious. This is true whether the relationship is brief or long, formal or informal.

Some of the major dynamics of personality which operate on the unconscious level are projection, sublimation, rationalization, and repression. Encountering these for the first time, one is apt to think of them as representing pathological states. In the extreme, they undoubtedly are, but they exist so universally that we must consider them also to be parts of normal personality.

Without necessarily subscribing to any of the numerous theories of personality, it is possible to describe personality in terms of certain important aspects or elements. We are all aware of ourselves as thinking organisms.

This aspect of personality, the conscious part, is important for understanding human behavior, but it is not enough. Many find it hard to accept the notion that each person also has an unconscious. The existence of the unconscious is no longer a matter of debate. It is not possible to estimate at all precisely What proportion of our total psychological life is conscious, what proportion unconscious. Everyone who has studied the problem, however, agrees that consciousness is the smaller part of personality. Most of what we are and do is a result of unconscious processes. To ignore this is to risk mistakes.

14. The passage above suggests that an interviewer can be MOST effective if he

    A. learns how to determine other peoples' unconscious motivations
    B. learns how to repress his own unconsciously motivated mannerisms and behavior
    C. can keep others from feeling that he either likes or dislikes them
    D. gains an understanding of how the unconscious operates in himself and in others

15. It may be inferred from the passage above that the *subtle processes such as gestures, posture, voice intonation, or choice of words* referred to in the first paragraph are USUALLY

    A. in the complete control of an expert investigator
    B. the determining factors in the friendships a person establishes
    C. controlled by a person's unconscious
    D. not capable of being consciously controlled

16. The passage above implies that various different personality theories are USUALLY

    A. so numerous and different as to be valueless to an investigator
    B. in basic agreement about the importance of the unconscious
    C. understood by the investigator who strives to be effective
    D. in agreement that personality factors such as projection and repression are pathological

Questions 17-19.

DIRECTIONS: Questions 17 through 19 are to be answered SOLELY on the basis of information contained in the following passage.

No matter how well the interrogator adjusts himself to the witness and how precisely he induces the witness to describe his observations, mistakes still can be made. The mistakes made by an experienced interrogator may be comparatively few, but as far as the witness is concerned, his path is full of pitfalls. Modern "witness psychology" has shown that even the most honest and trustworthy witnesses are apt to make grave mistakes in good faith. It is, therefore, necessary that the interrogator, get an idea of the weak links in the testimony in order to check up on them in the event that something appears to be strange or not quite satisfactory.

Unfortunately, modern witness psychology does not yet offer any means of directly testing the credibility of testimony. It lacks precision and method, in spite of worthwhile attempts on the part of learned men. At the same time, witness psychology, through the gathering of many experiences concerning the weaknesses of human testimony, has been of invaluable service. It shows clearly that only evidence of a technical nature has absolute value as proof.

Testimony may be separated into the following stages: (1) perception; (2) observation; (3) mind fixation of the observed occurrences, in which fantasy, association of ideas, and personal judgment participate; (4) expression in oral or written form, where the testimony is transferred from one witness to another or to the interrogator.

Each of these stages offers innumerable possibilities for the distortion of testimony.

17. The passage above indicates that having witnesses talk to each other before testifying is a practice which is GENERALLY

    A. *desirable*, since the witnesses will be able to correct each other's errors in observation before testimony
    B. *undesirable*, since the witnesses will collaborate on one story to tell the investigator
    C. *undesirable*, since one witness may distort his testimony because of what another witness may erroneously say
    D. *desirable*, since witnesses will become aware of discrepancies in their own testimony and can point out the discrepancies to the investigator

18. According to the above passage, the one of the following which would be the MOST reliable for use as evidence would be the testimony of a

    A. handwriting expert about a signature on a forged check
    B. trained police officer about the identity of a criminal
    C. laboratory technician about an accident he has observed
    D. psychologist who has interviewed any witnesses who relate conflicting stories

19. Concerning the validity of evidence, it is clear from the above passage that

    A. only evidence of a technical nature is at all valuable
    B. the testimony of witnesses is so flawed that it is usually valueless
    C. an investigator, by knowing modern witness psychology, will usually be able to perceive mistaken testimony
    D. an investigator ought to expect mistakes in even the most reliable witness testimony

Questions 20-21.

DIRECTIONS: Answer Questions 20 and 21 SOLELY on the basis of information given in the passage below.

Since we generally assure informants that what they say is confidential, we are not free to tell one informant what the other has told us. Even if the informant says, "I don't care who knows it; tell anybody you want to," we find it wise to treat the interview as confidential. An interviewer who relates to some informants what other informants have told him is likely to stir up anxiety and suspicion. Of course, the interviewer may be able to tell an informant what he has heard without revealing the source of his information. This may be perfectly appropriate where a story has wide currency so that an informant cannot infer the source of the information. *But if an event is not widely known, the mere mention of it may reveal to one informant what another informant has said about the situation. How can the data be cross-checked in these circumstances?*

20. The passage above IMPLIES that the anxiety and suspicion an interviewer may arouse by telling what has been learned in other interviews is due to the

    A. lack of trust the person interviewed may have in the interviewer's honesty
    B. troublesome nature of the material which the interviewer has learned in other interviews
    C. fact that the person interviewed may not believe that permission was given to repeat the information
    D. fear of the person interviewed that what he is telling the interviewer will be repeated

20.____

21. The paragraph above is MOST likely part of a longer passage dealing with

    A. ways to verify data gathered in interviews
    B. the various anxieties a person being interviewed may feel
    C. the notion that people sometimes say things they do not mean
    D. ways an interviewer can avoid seeming suspicious

21.____

Questions 22-23.

DIRECTIONS: Answer Questions 22 and 23 SOLELY on the basis of information given below.

The ability to interview rests not on any single trait, but on a vast complex of them. Habits, skills, techniques, and attitudes are all involved. Competence in interviewing is acquired only after careful and diligent study, prolonged practice (preferably under supervision), and a good bit of trial and error; for interviewing is not an exact science, it is an art. Like many other arts, however, it can and must draw on science in several of its aspects.

There is always a place for individual initiative, for imaginative innovations, and for new combinations of old approaches. The skilled interviewer cannot be bound by a set of rules. Likewise, there is not a set of rules which can guarantee to the novice that his interviewing will be successful. There are, however, some accepted, general guideposts which may help the beginner to avoid mistakes, learn how to conserve his efforts, and establish effective working relationships with interviewees; to accomplish, in short, what he sets out to do.

22. According to the passage above, rules and standard techniques for interviewing are

    A. helpful for the beginner, but useless for the experienced, innovative interviewer
    B. destructive of the innovation and initiative needed for a good interviewer
    C. useful for even the experienced interviewer, who may, however, sometimes go beyond them
    D. the means by which nearly anybody can become an effective interviewer

22.____

23. According to the passage above, the one of the following which is a prerequisite to competent interviewing is

    A. avoid mistakes   B. study and practice
    C. imaginative innovation   D. natural aptitude

23.____

Questions 24-27.

DIRECTIONS: Answer Questions 24 through 27 SOLELY on the basis of information given in the following paragraph.

The question of what material is relevant is not as simple as it might seem. Frequently, material which seems irrelevant to the inexperienced has, because of the common tendency to disguise and distort and misplace one's feelings, considerable significance. It may be necessary to let the client "ramble on" for a while in order to clear the decks, as it were, so that he may get down to things that really are on his mind. On the other hand, with an already disturbed person, it may be important for the interviewer to know when to discourage further elaboration of upsetting material. This is especially the case where the worker would be unable to do anything about it. An inexperienced interviewer might, for instance, be intrigued with the bizarre elaboration of material that the psychotic produces, but further elaboration of this might encourage the client in his instability. A too random discussion may indicate that the interviewee is not certain in what areas the interviewer is prepared to help him, and he may be seeking some direction. Or again, satisfying though it may be for the interviewer to have the interviewee tell him intimate details, such revelations sometimes need to be checked or encouraged only in small doses. An interviewee who has "talked too much" often reveals subsequent anxiety. This is illustrated by the fact that frequently after a "confessional" interview, the interviewee surprises the interviewer by being withdrawn, inarticulate, or hostile, or by breaking the next appointment.

24. Sometimes a client may reveal certain personal information to an interviewer and subsequently may feel anxious about this revelation.
If, during an interview, a client begins to discuss very personal matters, it would be BEST to

    A. tell the client, in no uncertain terms, that you're not interested in personal details
    B. ignore the client at this point
    C. encourage the client to elaborate further on the details
    D. inform the client that the information seems to be very personal

25. The author indicates that clients with severe psychological disturbances pose an especially difficult problem for the inexperienced interviewer.
The difficulty lies in the possibility of the client

    A. becoming physically violent and harming the interviewer
    B. *rambling on* for a while
    C. revealing irrelevant details which may be followed by cancelled appointments
    D. reverting to an unstable state as a result of interview material

26. An interviewer should be constantly alert to the possibility of obtaining clues from the client as to the problem areas.
According to the above passage, a client who discusses topics at random may be

    A. unsure of what problems the interviewer can provide help with
    B. reluctant to discuss intimate details
    C. trying to impress the interviewer with his knowledge
    D. deciding what relevant material to elaborate on

27. The evaluation of a client's responses may reveal substantial information that may aid the interviewer in assessing the problem areas that are of concern to the client. Responses that seemed irrelevant at the time of the interview may be of significance because

    A. considerable significance is attached to all irrelevant material
    B. emotional feelings are frequently masked
    C. an initial *rambling on* is often a prelude to what is actually bothering the client
    D. disturbed clients often reveal subsequent anxiety

27.____

Questions 28-30.

DIRECTIONS: Answer Questions 28 through 30 SOLELY on the basis of the following paragraph.

The physical setting of the interview may determine its entire potentiality. Some degree of privacy and a comfortable relaxed atmosphere are important. The interviewee is not encouraged to give much more than his name and address if the interviewer seems busy with other things, if people are rushing about, if there are distracting noises. He has a right to feel that, whether the interview lasts five minutes or an hour, he has, for that time, the undivided attention of the interviewer. Interruptions, telephone calls, and so on, should be reduced to a minimum. If the interviewee has waited in a crowded room for what seems to him an interminably long period, he is naturally in no mood to sit down and discuss what is on his mind. Indeed, by that time, the primary thing on his mind may be his irritation at being kept waiting, and he frequently feels it would be impolite to express this. If a wait or interruptions have been unavoidable, it is always helpful to give the client some recognition that these are disturbing and that we can naturally understand that they make it more difficult for him to proceed. At the same time, if he protests that they have not troubled him, the interviewer can best accept his statements at their face value, as further insistence that they must have been disturbing may be interpreted by him as accusing, and he may conclude that the interviewer has been personally hurt by his irritation.

28. Distraction during an interview may tend to limit the client's responses.
    In a case where an interruption has occurred, it would be BEST for the investigator to

    A. terminate this interview and have it rescheduled for another time period
    B. ignore the interruption since it is not continuous
    C. express his understanding that the distraction can cause the client to feel disturbed
    D. accept the client's protests that he has been troubled by the interruption

28.____

29. To maximize the rapport that can be established with the client, an appropriate physical setting is necessary. At the very least, some privacy would be necessary.
    In addition, the interviewer should

    A. always appear to be busy in order to impress the client
    B. focus his attention only on the client
    C. accept all the client's statements as being valid
    D. stress the importance of the interview to the client

29.____

30. Clients who have been waiting quite some time for their interview may, justifiably, become upset.
However, a client may initially attempt to mask these feelings because he may

    A. personally hurt the interviewer
    B. want to be civil
    C. feel that the wait was unavoidable
    D. fear the consequences of his statement

30._____

KEY (CORRECT ANSWERS)

1. B	11. A	21. A
2. C	12. B	22. C
3. D	13. D	23. B
4. D	14. D	24. D
5. B	15. C	25. D
6. D	16. B	26. A
7. C	17. C	27. B
8. C	18. A	28. C
9. D	19. D	29. B
10. C	20. D	30. B

TEST 2

DIRECTIONS: Each question or incomplete statement is followed by several suggested answers or completions. Select the one that BEST answers the question or completes the statement. *PRINT THE LETTER OF THE CORRECT ANSWER IN THE SPACE AT THE RIGHT.*

Questions 1-5.

DIRECTIONS In Questions 1 through 5, choose the sentence which is BEST from the point of view of English usage suitable for a business report.

1. A. The client's receiving of public assistance checks at two different addresses were disclosed by the investigation.
    B. The investigation disclosed that the client was receiving public assistance checks at two different addresses.
    C. The client was found out by the investigation to be receiving public assistance checks at two different addresses.
    D. The client has been receiving public assistance checks at two different addresses, disclosed the investigation.

    1._____

2. A. The investigation of complaints are usually handled by this unit, which deals with internal security problems in the department.
    B. This unit deals with internal security problems in the department; usually investigating complaints.
    C. Investigating complaints is this unit's job, being that it handles internal security problems in the department.
    D. This unit deals with internal security problems in the department and usually investigates complaints.

    2._____

3. A. The delay in completing this investigation was caused by difficulty in obtaining the required documents from the candidate.
    B. Because of difficulty in obtaining the required documents from the candidate is the reason that there was a delay in completing this investigation.
    C. Having had difficulty in obtaining the required documents from the candidate, there was a delay in completing this investigation.
    D. Difficulty in obtaining the required documents from the candidate had the affect of delaying the completion of this investigation.

    3._____

4. A. This report, together with documents supporting our recommendation, are being submitted for your approval.
    B. Documents supporting our recommendation is being submitted with the report for your approval.
    C. This report, together with documents supporting our recommendation, is being submitted for your approval.
    D. The report and documents supporting our recommendation is being submitted for your approval.

    4._____

5.
- A. Several people were interviewed and numerous letters were sent before this case was completed.
- B. Completing this case, interviewing several people and sending numerous letters were necessary.
- C. To complete this case needed interviewing several people and sending numerous letters.
- D. Interviewing several people and sending numerous letters was necessary to complete the case.

Questions 6-20.

DIRECTIONS: For each of the sentences numbered 6 to 20, select from the options given below the MOST applicable choice, and mark your answer accordingly.
- A. The sentence is correct.
- B. The sentence contains a spelling error only.
- C. The sentence contains an English grammar error only.
- D. The sentence contains both a spelling error and an English grammar error.

6. He is a very dependible person whom we expect will be an asset to this division.

7. An investigator often finds it necessary to be very diplomatic when conducting an interview.

8. Accurate detail is especially important if court action results from an investigation.

9. The report was signed by him and I since we conducted the investigation jointly.

10. Upon receipt of the complaint, an inquiry was begun.

11. An employee has to organize his time so that he can handle his workload efficiantly.

12. It was not apparant that anyone was living at the address given by the client.

13. According to regulations, there is to be at least three attempts made to locate the client.

14. Neither the inmate nor the correction officer was willing to sign a formal statement.

15. It is our opinion that one of the persons interviewed were lying.

16. We interviewed both clients and departmental personel in the course of this investigation.

17. It is concievable that further research might produce additional evidence.

18. There are too many occurences of this nature to ignore.

19. We cannot accede to the candidate's request.

20. The submission of overdue reports is the reason that there was a delay in completion of this investigation.

Questions 21-25.

DIRECTIONS: Each of Questions 21 to 25 consists of three sentences lettered A, B, and C. In each of these questions, one of the sentences may contain an error in grammar, sentence structure, or punctuation, or all three sentences may be correct. If one of the sentences in a question contains an error in grammar, sentence structure, or punctuation, print in the space on the right the capital letter preceding the sentence which contains the error. If all three sentences are correct, print the letter D.

21. A. Mr. Smith appears to be less competent than I in performing these duties.
    B. The supervisor spoke to the employee, who had made the error, but did not reprimand him.
    C. When he found the book lying on the table, he immediately notified the owner.

    21._____

22. A. Being locked in the desk, we were certain that the papers would not be taken.
    B. It wasn't I who dictated the telegram; I believe it was Eleanor.
    C. You should interview whoever comes to the office today.

    22._____

23. A. The clerk was instructed to set the machine on the table before summoning the manager.
    B. He said that he was not familiar with those kind of activities.
    C. A box of pencils, in addition to erasers and blotters, was included in the shipment of supplies.

    23._____

24. A. The supervisor remarked, "Assigning an employee to the proper type of work is not always easy."
    B. The employer found that each of the applicants were qualified to perform the duties of the position.
    C. Any competent student is permitted to take this course if he obtains the consent of the instructor.

    24._____

25. A. The prize was awarded to the employee whom the judges believed to be most deserving.
    B. Since the instructor believes this book is the better of the two, he is recommending it for use in the school.
    C. It was obvious to the employees that the completion of the task by the scheduled date would require their working overtime.

    25._____

KEY (CORRECT ANSWERS)

1.	B	11.	B
2.	D	12.	B
3.	A	13.	C
4.	C	14.	A
5.	A	15.	C
6.	D	16.	B
7.	A	17.	B
8.	A	18.	B
9.	C	19.	A
10.	A	20.	C

21. B
22. A
23. B
24. B
25. D

ARITHMETICAL REASONING
EXAMINATION SECTION
TEST 1

DIRECTIONS: Each question or incomplete statement is followed by several suggested answers or completions. Select the one that BEST answers the question or completes the statement. *PRINT THE LETTER OF THE CORRECT ANSWER IN THE SPACE AT THE RIGHT.*

1. Liquid toilet soap is supplied in 5-gallon cans. If each of the twelve toilet rooms in your building uses an average of one quart of toilet soap per month, the amount of cans you should be required to requisite to cover needs for a three month period is

    A. two B. three C. four D. five

    1._____

2. A corridor is ten feet wide and 210 feet long. If it takes a two-man crew about one hour to mop 5,000 square feet, the amount of time required for mopping the corridor is MOST NEARLY_____ minutes.

    A. 30 B. 25
    C. 15 D. 10

    2._____

3. If 75 crates of food were ordered and 100 crates were delivered, then the shipment is larger than the number ordered by _____ crates.

    A. 10 B. 15 C. 25 D. 35

    3._____

4. If 200 boxes of merchandise were ordered and 100 boxes are delivered, then the shipment is short by _____ boxes.

    A. 50 B. 100 C. 150 D. 175

    4._____

5. You are to load a hand truck with cartons weighing a total of 200 pounds.
    If each carton weighs 20 pounds, then the TOTAL number of cartons to be loaded is

    A. 8 B. 9 C. 10 D. 11

    5._____

6. You are to unpack twelve cartons of paper and place the paper on a storage shelf.
    If each carton has eight packs of paper, then the number of packs of paper that you will place on the shelf is

    A. 72 B. 84 C. 96 D. 108

    6._____

7. If floor wax costs $2.90 a gallon, then the TOTAL cost of a carton in which there are six gallons of wax is

    A. $17.40 B. $19.00 C. $21.40 D. $29.00

    7._____

8. You know that a storage shelf unit can safely hold items up to a total weight of 300 pounds.
    If there are already 8 boxes of canned food on the shelves of the unit, all exactly the same, and each box weighs 25 pounds, then the number of the same boxes of canned food that you can safely add to those on the shelves is

    A. 4 B. 5 C. 6 D. 7

    8._____

9. During the month of June, 40,587 people attended a city-owned swimming pool. In July, 13,014 more people attended the swimming pool than the number that had attended in June. In August, 39,655 people attended the swimming pool. The TOTAL number of people who attended the swimming pool during the months of June, July, and August was

   A. 80,242 B. 93,256 C. 133,843 D. 210,382

   9._____

10. Assume that your agency has been given $2,025 to purchase file cabinets.
    If each file cabinet costs $135, how many file cabinets can your agency purchase?

    A. 8 B. 10 C. 15 D. 16

    10._____

11. Assume that your unit ordered 14 staplers at a total cost of $30.20, and each stapler cost the same.
    The cost of one stapler was MOST NEARLY

    A. $1.02 B. $1.61 C. $2.16 D. $2.26

    11._____

12. Assume that you are responsible for counting and recording licensing fees collected by your department. On a particular day, your department collected in fees 40 checks in the amount of $6 each, 80 checks in the amount of $4 each, 45 twenty dollar bills, 30 ten dollar bills, 42 five dollar bills, and 186 one dollar bills.
    The TOTAL amount in fees collected on that day was

    A. $1,406 B. $1,706 C. $2,156 D. $2,356

    12._____

13. Assume that you are responsible for your agency's petty cash fund. During the month of February, you pay out 7 subway fares at 50? each and one taxi fare for $2.85. You pay out nothing else from the fund. At the end of February, you count the money left in the fund and find 3 one dollar bills, 4 quarters, 5 dimes, and 4 nickels. The amount of money you had available in the petty cash fund at the BEGINNING of February was

    A. $4.70 B. $6.35 C. $7.55 D. $11.05

    13._____

14. Assume that you are assigned to sell tickets at a city-owned ice skating rink. An adult ticket costs $1.50, and a children's ticket costs $.75. At the end of a day, you find that you have sold 36 adult tickets and 80 children's tickets.
    The TOTAL amount of money you collected for that day was

    A. $81.60 B. $106.00 C. $114.00 D. $116.00

    14._____

15. If each office worker files 487 index cards in one hour, how many cards can 26 office workers file in one hour?

    A. 10,662 B. 12,175 C. 12,662 D. 14,266

    15._____

16. Assume a city agency has 775 office workers.
    If 2 out of 25 office workers were absent on a particular day, how many office workers reported to work on that day?

    A. 713 B. 744 C. 750 D. 773

    16._____

17. If a worker earns $9.18 per hour and works a 40-hour week, his weekly pay will be

    A. $357.20 B. $366.20 C. $366.40 D. $367.20

    17._____

18. If a stock clerk earns $13.12 per hour and works a 40-hour week, how much will she receive in two weeks? 18._____

   A. $1,049.60
   B. $1,049.80
   C. $1,050.60
   D. $1,051.60

19. A stock clerk earns $9.18 per hour when he works a 40-hour week and is paid for overtime at time and a half for all time worked over 40 hours.
How much money for overtime should he receive if he worked a 48-hour week? 19._____

   A. $109.16   B. $109.28   C. $110.16   D. $110.36

20. The reorder quantity is reached by multiplying the average monthly usage by the lead time (in months) and adding the minimum balance. For a particular item, the lead time is 2 months, the minimum balance is 100, and the average monthly usage is 150.
The reorder quantity for this item is 20._____

   A. 300   B. 400   C. 600   D. 1,000

21. If a job can be completed by 4 employees in 6 days, how many days will it take 6 employees working at an equal speed to do the same job? 21._____

   A. 2   B. 3   C. 3 1/2   D. 4

22. If your rate of pay is $8.00 an hour for a 40-hour work week, and in an emergency you volunteer to work your half-hour lunch period for 5 days at straight time, what will your TOTAL gross pay be at the end of the week? 22._____

   A. $340   B. $350   C. $370   D. $380

23. If the gross weight of a trailer truck with a load of ferrous scrap removed from your storage yard is 67,130 pounds and the tare weight is 24,570 pounds, what is the weight, in gross tons, of the scrap removed? 23._____

   A. 17   B. 18   C. 19   D. 21

24. You receive a requisition for 2 1/2 gross of machine screws. The number of machine screws you should dispense is 24._____

   A. 300   B. 324   C. 360   D. 400

25. A requisition for a ream of paper is a request for how many sheets of paper? 25._____

   A. 200   B. 500   C. 750   D. 1,000

KEY (CORRECT ANSWERS)

1.	A	11.	C
2.	B	12.	C
3.	C	13.	D
4.	B	14.	C
5.	C	15.	C
6.	C	16.	A
7.	A	17.	D
8.	A	18.	A
9.	C	19.	C
10.	C	20.	B

21. D
22. A
23. D
24. C
25. B

5 (#1)

SOLUTIONS TO PROBLEMS

1. (12)(1 qt.) = 12 qts. = 3 gallons per month. For 3 months, 9 gallons are needed. Since the soap is supplied in 5-gallon cans, 2 cans are required.

2. (10')(210') = 2100 sq.ft. Time required = (2100/5000) hrs. = .42 hrs. - 25 min. (Closest answer given is 30 min.)

3. 100 - 75 = 25 crates

4. 200 - 100 = 100 boxes

5. 200 20 = 10 cartons

6. (12) (8) = 96 packs of paper

7. ($2.90)(6) = $17.40

8. Maximum allowable number of boxes = 300 ÷ 25 = 12. Since there are already 8 boxes on the shelves, 4 more may be added.

9. Total number of people = 40,587 + 53,601 + 39,655 = 133,843

10. $2025 $135 = 15 file cabinets

11. $30.20 14 = $2.16 per stapler

12. (40)($6) + (80)($4) + (45)($20) + (30)($10) + (42)($5) + (186)($1) = $2156

13. (7)($.50) + (1)($2.85) + (3)($1) + (4)($.25) + (5)($.10) + (4)($.05) = $11.05

14. (36)($1.50) + (80)($.75) = $114.00

15. (26)(487) = 12,662 cards

16. 16. Since 23 out of 25 were present, this represents .92 of these workers. Then, (.92)(775) = 713

17. ($9.18)(40) = $367.20

18. ($13.12)(40)(2) = $1049.60

19. ($9.18)(40) + ($13.77)(8) = $477.36 total, but his overtime is (13.77)(8) = $110.16

20. Reorder quantity = (150)(2) + 100 = 400

21. (4)(6) = 24 employee-days. Then, 24 ÷ 6 = 4 days

22. ($8.00)(40) + ($8.00)(2.5) = $340

6 (#1)

23. 67,130 - 24,570 = 42,560 lbs. 2,000 = 21.28 tons = 21 tons

24. (2 1/2)(144) = 360 machine screws

25. 1 ream = 500 sheets of paper

TEST 2

DIRECTIONS: Each question or incomplete statement is followed by several suggested answers or completions. Select the one that BEST answers the question or completes the statement. *PRINT THE LETTER OF THE CORRECT ANSWER IN THE SPACE AT THE RIGHT.*

1. A bin in your storeroom measuring 2' x 1.5' x 4' has a storage volume of _____ cubic feet.

    A. 12   B. 24   C. 50   D. 72

2. A gill is equivalent to 8 fluid ounces.
   How many gills are required to fill a 5-gallon container with distilled water?

    A. 70   B. 75   C. 80   D. 85

3. A storage space 8'6" wide and 9'6" long has an area that is CLOSEST to _____ square feet.

    A. 80   B. 81   C. 82   D. 83

4. A drill bit has a diameter of 13/32 inch.
   Of the following, the decimal number CLOSEST to 13/32 is

    A. 0.406   B. 0.408   C. 0.410   D. 0.412

5. If repaired units come into your storeroom in a palletized container indicating that the gross weight is 2250 pounds, then the

    A. container alone weighs 2250 pounds
    B. repaired units alone weigh 2250 pounds
    C. repaired units and palletized container weigh 2250 pounds
    D. weight of 2250 pounds is approximate

6. You have 5 pieces of lumber. Their lengths are: 8'2", 6'4", 3'4", 5'9", and 4'5".
   What is the sum of the lengths of the 5 pieces of lumber?

    A. 26'   B. 26'9"   C. 27'10"   D. 28'

7. A full reel of 1,000 feet of power distribution cable weighs 8,095 pounds. The cable weighs 7.6 pounds per foot. The weight of the empty reel is _____ pounds.

    A. 465   B. 480   C. 495   D. 510

8. A crate 2' by 3' by 6' has a volume of _____ cubic yards.

    A. 6   B. 1 1/3   C. 18   D. 4

9. Of 600 pieces received in a shipment, 50 are inspected. Of the 50, 10 are found damaged.
   If the 50 are a representative sampling, the number of items in the entire shipment LIKELY to be damaged is

    A. 50   B. 60   C. 80   D. 120

10. A board having 3 square feet has how many square inches?

    A. 144 B. 288 C. 432 D. 576

11. A crate of material delivered to your storeroom has inscribed on it the words *Net Weight 250 pounds*.
    This means that the

    A. weight of 250 pounds is approximate
    B. material and crate together weigh 250 pounds
    C. material alone weighs 250 pounds
    D. crate alone weighs 250 pounds

12. A box contains an equal number of brass and copper tubes. Each brass tube weighs 4 pounds, each copper tube weighs 1 pound, and the empty box weighs 5 pounds. The total weight of the box and tubes is 200 pounds.
    The TOTAL number of tubes in the box is

    A. 39 B. 60 C. 78 D. 156

13. A caretaker received $70.00 for having worked from Monday through Friday, 9 M. to 5 P.M., with one hour a day for lunch.
    The number of hours the caretaker would have to work to earn $12.00 is

    A. 10
    B. 6
    C. 70 divided by 12
    D. 70 minus 12

14. If the cost of a broom went up from $4.00 to $6.00, the percent INCREASE in the original cost is

    A. 20 B. 25 C. 33 1/3 D. 50

15. The AVERAGE of the numbers 3, 5, 7, 8, 12 is

    A. 5 B. 6 C. 7 D. 8

16. The cost of 100 bags of cotton cleaning cloths, 89 pounds per bag, at 7 cents per pound, is

    A. $549.35 B. $623.00 C. $700.00 D. $890.00

17. If 5 1/2 bags of sweeping compound cost $55.00, then 6 1/2 bags would cost

    A. $60.00 B. $62.50 C. $65.00 D. $67.00

18. The cost of cleaning supplies in a project averaged $330.00 a month during the first 8 months of the year. How much can be spent each month for the last four months if the total amount that can be spent for cleaning supplies for the year is $3,880?

    A. $124.00 B. $220.00 C. $310.00 D. $330.00

19. A shelf in a supply closet can safely hold only 100 pounds. A package of paper towels weighs 2 pounds, a carton of disinfectant weighs 8 pounds, and a box of soap weighs 1 pound. There are already 6 cartons of disinfectant and 6 boxes of soap on the shelf. How many packages of towels can be SAFELY placed there?

    A. 20 B. 23 C. 25 D. 27

20. A cleaning solution is made up of 4 gallons of water, 1 pint of liquid soap, and 1 pint of ammonia.
    How many gallons of water are needed to use up a gallon of ammonia?

    A. 8   B. 16   C. 24   D. 32

21. Suppose a caretaker has 50 stair halls to clean. If he cleans 74% of them, the number of stair halls still UNCLEANED is

    A. 38   B. 26   C. 24   D. 13

22. If a man has a 12 foot piece of wood and wishes to cut it into two pieces so that one piece is twice as long as the other, the LONGER piece should be _____ feet.

    A. 7   B. 7 1/2   C. 8   D. 8 1/2

23. If fuel oil costs $1.09 9/10 per gallon, and $224 was the total cost for a tank fill-up, how many gallons were delivered?

    A. 203.82   B. 190.59   C. 217.38   D. 179.97

24. A drill bit has a diameter of 17/36". Of the following, the decimal equivalent CLOSEST to 17/36 is

    A. 0.444   B. 0.531   C. 0.473   D. 0.472

25. If cleaning solution costs $1.53 per gallon, what is the TOTAL cost of 2 cartons of cleaning solution when each carton holds 12 one-gallon jugs?

    A. $36.24   B. $36.72   C. $39.12   D. $37.92

KEY (CORRECT ANSWERS)

1.	A	11.	C
2.	C	12.	C
3.	B	13.	B
4.	A	14.	D
5.	C	15.	C
6.	D	16.	B
7.	C	17.	C
8.	B	18.	C
9.	D	19.	B
10.	C	20.	D

21. D
22. C
23. A
24. D
25. B

5 (#2)

SOLUTIONS TO PROBLEMS

1. Volume = (21)(1.5')(4') = 12 cu.ft.

2. 5 gallons = (128)(5) = 640 fluid oz. Then, 640 8 = 80 gills

3. Area = (8'6")(9'6") = (8.5')(9.5') = 80.75 = 81 sq.ft.

4. 13/32 = .40625 = .406

5. Gross weight = combined weight of repaired units and palletized container.

6. 8'2" + 6'4" + 3'4" + 5'9" + 4'5" = 26'24" = 28'

7. Empty reel weight = 8095 - (7.6)(1000) = 495 lbs.

8. (2')(3')(6') = 36 cu.ft. = 36/27 = 1 1/2 cu.yds.

9. 10/50 = 20%. Then, (20%)(600) = 120 are likely to be damaged.

10. 3 sq.ft. = (3)(144) = 432 sq.in.

11. Net weight refers to the contents of the crate, not including the crate's weight.

12. Let x = number of brass and copper tubes together. Then, $(1/2x)(4) + (1/2)(1) + 5 = 200$. Simplifying, we get $2.5x = 195$. Solving, $x = 78$

13. $70 is paid for (7)(5) = 35 hrs., which means $2 per hour. Thus, $12 is received in 12/2 = 6 hours.

14. Percent increase = ($2.00/$4.00)(100) = 50%

15. Average = (3+5+7+8+12)/5 = 35/5 = 7

16. Cost = (100)(89)($.07) = $623.00

17. $55 ÷ 5.5 = $10 per bag. Then, 6 1/2 bags cost (6 1/2)($10) = $65.00

18. Let x = amount spent during each of the last 4 months. Then, $(8)($330) + 4x = 3880. Solving, $x = 310.00

19. Let x = number of pkgs. of towels. Then, $2x + (6)(8) + (6)(1) = 100$. Simplifying, $2x = 46$. Solving, $x = 23$

20. Since 1 gallon = 8 pints, 1 gallon of ammonia requires (4)(8) = 32 gallons of water

21. Number of stair halls uncleaned = (.26)(50) = 13

22. Let x = longer piece, $1/2x$ = shorter piece. Then, $x + 1/2x = 12$. Solving, $x = 8$ ft.

6 (#2)

23. $224 ÷ $1.099 ≈ 203.82 gallons

24. $17/36 = .47\overline{2} ≈ .472$

25. Total cost = (2)(12)($1.53) = $36.72

TEST 3

DIRECTIONS: Each question or Incomplete statement is followed by several suggested answers or completions. Select the one that BEST answers the question or completes the statement. *PRINT THE LETTER OF THE CORRECT ANSWER IN THE SPACE AT THE RIGHT.*

1. A storeroom is 100 feet long and 26 feet wide. One aisle 8 feet wide runs the length of the storeroom.
   One aisle 4 feet wide runs the width of the storeroom. If there were no other aisles, the number of square feet of usable storage space would be

   A. 1696   B. 1728   C. 2280   D. 2568

2. A discount of 1% is given on all purchases of a certain item In quantities of 100 units or more. An additional discount of 1% is given on that portion of the purchase which exceeds 300.
   If 450 units are purchased at a list price of $6.00, the total cost is

   A. $2,619   B. $2,664   C. $2,670   D. $2,682

3. The number of cartons measuring 3'x3'x2' which will be needed to pack 1,728 boxed Items each measuring 3"x9"x6" is

   A. 9   B. 18   C. 108   D. 192

4. A space 5 1/2 feet wide and 2 1/3 feet long has an area measured MOST NEARLY _____ square feet.

   A. 9   B. 10   C. 11   D. 12

5. One man is able to load two 2 1/2 ton trucks In one hour. To load ten such trucks, it will take ten men _____ hour(s).

   A. 1/2   B. 1   C. 2   D. 2 1/2

6. If the average height of the stacks In your section of the storehouse is 10', the area which will be occupied by 56,000 cubic feet of supplies, is MOST LIKELY to be

   A. 70'x80'   B. 60'x90'   C. 50'x60'   D. 560'x100'

7. The number of cartons, each measuring two cubic feet, which can fit into a space which is 100 square feet in area and Is 8' high is

   A. 50   B. 200   C. 400   D. 800

8. When the floor area measures 200' by 200' and the maximum weight it can hold is 4,000 tons, then the safe floor load is _____ pounds per square foot.

   A. 20   B. 160   C. 200   D. 400

9. A carton 1' x 1' x 3' measures _____ cubic yard(s).

   A. 1/3   B. 1/9   C. 3   D. 9

10. You have received 6 cartons, each containing 60 boxes of staples, priced at $36.00 per carton.
The price per box is

    A. $.10 B. $.60 C. $3.60 D. $6.00

11. The amount of space in cubic feet, required to store 100 boxes each, measuring 24" x 12" x 6", is

    A. 10 B. 100 C. 168 D. 1,008

12. Assume that it takes an average of 2 man-hours to stack 1 ton of certain supplies.
In order to stack 30 tons, the number of men required to complete the job in ten hours is

    A. 6 B. 10 C. 15 D. 30

13. An area measures 20'x22 1/2'. The floor load is 100 lbs. per square foot.
The total weight that can be stored in this area is MOST NEARLY _____ lbs.

    A. 450 B. 9,000 C. 22,500 D. 45,000

14. The price of a certain type of linoleum is $1.00 per square foot.
The total cost of four pieces of 9'x12' linoleum is MOST NEARLY

    A. $105 B. $400 C. $430 D. $2,160

15. The number of board feet in a piece of lumber measuring 2" thick by 2' wide by 12' long is

    A. 12 B. 16 C. 24 D. 48

KEY (CORRECT ANSWERS)

1. B	6. A	11. B
2. B	7. C	12. A
3. A	8. C	13. D
4. D	9. B	14. C
5. A	10. B	15. D

SOLUTIONS TO PROBLEMS

1. (26-8)(100-4) = 1728 sq.ft. of usable space

2. 300 1% @ $5.94 = $1782; 150 2% @ $5.88 = $882. $1782 + $882 = $2664

3. (3' 3')(3' 9")(2' 6") = (12)(4)(4) = 192 boxes per carton Then, 1728 192 = 9 cartons

4. (5 1/4')(2 1/3') = 12 1/4 sq.ft. = 12 sq.ft.

5. One man could load 10 trucks in 5 hrs. Thus, 10 men would need 5/10 = 1/2 hr. to load these 10 trucks.

6. 56,000 ÷ 10' = 5600 sq.ft. Selection A which is 70'x80' would yield 5600 sq.ft.

7. (100)(8) = 800 cu.ft., and 800 2 = 400

8. (200')(200') = 40,000 sq.ft. Then, (4000)(2000) 40,000 = 200 lbs. per sq.ft.

9. (1')(1')(3') = 3 cu.ft. = 3/27 = 1/9 cu.yd.

10. $36.00 60 = $.60 per box

11. (100)(2')(1')(1/2') = 100 cu.ft.

12. 30 tons requires (2) (30) = 60 man-hours. Then, 60 10 = 6 men.

13. (100)(20')(22 1/2) = 45,000 lbs.

14. ($1.00)(9')(12')(4) = $432 = $430

15. Each side of board = (2')(12') = 24 sq.ft. Total area = (2) (24) = 48 sq.ft.

ARITHMETICAL REASONING
EXAMINATION SECTION
TEST 1

DIRECTIONS: Each question or incomplete statement is followed by several suggested answers or completions. Select the one that BEST answers the question or completes the statement. *PRINT THE LETTER OF THE CORRECT ANSWER IN THE SPACE AT THE RIGHT.*

1. The initial mark-up in a store is 40%; mark-downs are 5%; shortages 1%; cash discounts 5%; alteration costs 5%; expenses 25%.
   The maintained mark-up is

   A. 34%   B. 39%   C. 36.4%   D. 30%

   1._____

2. A buyer of TV sets wishes to maintain a mark-up of 37 1/2% after all mark-downs are taken. Of 25 sets costing $150 each, he sells 20 at $265.
   How much can he mark-down the remaining 5 sets and still realize his mark-up objective?

   A. $166   B. $150   C. $140   D. $125

   2._____

3. An article originally selling for $12 and costing $8 was marked down to $10. Assuming the same markup,
   what is the present market value of its cost?

   A. $6.68   B. $8.00   C. $5.67   D. $6.86

   3._____

4. What is the *on* percentage of trade discounts of 20% and 10%?

   A. 70   B. 85   C. 72   D. 80

   4._____

5. Canadian cost of a sweater is $40. Packing and labor cost $5.00; ad valorem duty, 40%; specific duty, 65¢; rate of exchange, .9091.
   What is the duty in American currency?

   A. $16.96   B. $16.36   C. $18.00   D. $18.60

   5._____

6. A bolt of cloth measures 40 yards. The following yardages are sold: 4 1/2, 5 3/4, 6 7/8.
   How many yards are left?

   A. 23 7/8   B. 22 1/2   C. 22 7/8   D. 24 3/8

   6._____

7. A shirt manufacturer has 76 1/2 yards of broadcloth to be used for shirts.
   If each shirt takes 2 1/2 yards, how many shirts can he make?

   A. 38   B. 30   C. 19   D. 31

   7._____

8. Subtract 1.003 from 24.5.

   A. 24.003   B. 12.42   C. 23.2   D. 23.497

   8._____

2 (#1)

9. A store carries a stock amounting to $265,830.25. Cash discounts, on the average, amount to 5 1/4%.
   How much are the cash discounts?

   A. $13,956.09 B. $1,395.61
   C. $139.56   D. $1.39

   9.____

10. If the sales in a department totaled $67,507.50 and the average sale was $22.50, how many transactions were there?

    A. 3,000   B. 300   C. 30,000   D. 30

    10.____

11. A department store reports a decrease in sales of 5.5% for this year.
    If this year's sales are $275,825,000, last year's sales were

    A. $291,878,000   B. $290,995,000
    C. $260,655,000   D. $290,788,000

    11.____

12. For the current year, the sales volume in a store was $50,000,000. Other income amounted to $1,500,000, Operating expenses were $10,000,000; cost of goods sold, $37,500,000.
    What is the percent of net profit based on retail?

    A. 10   B. 8   C. 50   D. 13

    12.____

13. If this year's sales show an increase of 300% over last year, this year's sales are how many times last year's sales?

    A. 3   B. 1 1/3   C. 4   D. 1/4

    13.____

14. Net sales in a shop amounted to $374,000; returns were 10%; allowances, 5%.
    What were the gross sales?

    A. $430,100   B. $415,000   C. $411,400   D. $440,000

    14.____

15. If the average sale in a store is expected to rise 5% over last year, and the number of transactions increases 3%, what percentage of increase in dollar sales volume should be planned?

    A. 8   B. 4   C. 8.15   D. 8.51

    15.____

16. The billed cost on an invoice is $300; freight charges, $10; cash discount, 2%; the retail value of the merchandise is $525.
    The mark-up percent on retail is

    A. 40.9   B. 42   C. 69   D. 69.5

    16.____

17. A hat costing $30.00 is to be given a mark-up of 45% on retail.
    The retail should be

    A. $43.50   B. $46.40   C. $55.40   D. $54.50

    17.____

18. Retail price $40 per unit; mark-up 40% of retail; transportation charge $1 per unit.
    Find billed cost that store can pay.

    A. $23   B. $24   C. $23.75   D. $24.75

    18.____

19. A buyer plans to spend $17,000 at retail for merchandise at a mark-up of 34%. He finds 19.____
    a special value at $3,000 that he can sell for $6,000.
    What mark-up percentage does he need on the balance of his purchases in order to
    achieve his planned 34%?

    A. 35   B. 19.9   C. 15   D. 22.5

20. A store has a gross margin of 40% and reductions of 13%. Cash discount on purchases 20.____
    are not credited to the department. There are no alteration costs.
    What is the initial mark-up?

    A. 46%   B. 53%   C. 27%   D. 26%

21. A dress is to retail for $35 with a mark-up of 40% of retail. 21.____
    The cost of the dress to the retailer was

    A. $25   B. $21   C. $14   D. $20

22. The cost is $1.20 and the desired gross profit is 40% of retail. 22.____
    The retail price should be

    A. $1.60   B. $1.68   C. $2.00   D. $2.40

23. The realized mark-up on a TV set is $50. The mark-up is 25% of retail. 23.____
    The cost of the TV set to the retailer was

    A. $200   B. $125   C. $100   D. $150

24. Farnum, a salesman, earns $9.60 per hour for 40 hours a week, with time and a half for 24.____
    all hours over 40 per week. Last week, his total earnings were $470.40.
    How many hours did he work last week?

    A. 46   B. 49   C. 47   D. 48

25. Dane & Clarke, partners, share profits in a 5:3 ratio. Dane's share of the profit for this 25.____
    year was $12,000 more than Clarke's share.
    Clarke's share of the net profit was

    A. $30,000   B. $48,000   C. $36,000   D. $18,000

KEY (CORRECT ANSWERS)

1. C
2. D
3. A
4. C
5. A

6. C
7. B
8. D
9. A
10. A

11. A
12. B
13. C
14. D
15. C

16. A
17. D
18. A
19. B
20. A

21. B
22. C
23. D
24. A
25. D

SOLUTIONS TO PROBLEMS

1. $5 + 5 - 1 = 9\%$. Then, $(40\%)(.91) = 36.4\%$.

2. $(25)(\$150) = \$3750$ and $\$3750 \div .625 = \$6000$ total selling price of all sets. $\$6000 - (20)(\$265) = \$700$; $700 \div 5 = \$140$ selling price for each of the last 5 sets. Markdown amount = $\$265 - \$140 = \$125$

3. When the article's original selling price was $12, its cost was $8.00. If the article's original selling price were to be $10, it would cost $(8.00/12.00 \times 10.00) = \$6.67$

4. Resulting percentage = $(1-.20)(1-.10) = .72 = 72\%$

5. $(\$45)(.40) = \$18$, $18 + .65 = \$18.65$. Then, $(\$18.65)(.9091) = \$16.95$, closest to $16.96 in American currency.

6. $40 - 4\ 1/2 - 5\ 3/4 - 6\ 7/8 = 22\ 7/8$ yds.

7. $76\ 1/2 \div 2\ 1/2 = 30.6$, rounded down to 30 shirts

8. $24.5 - 1.003 = 23.497$

9. $(\$265,830.25)(.0525) = \$13,956.09$

10. $\$67,507.50 \div \$22.50 = 3000$ transactions

11. $\$275,825,000 \div .945 = \$291,878,000$

12. $\$50,000,000 + \$1,500,000 - \$10,000,000 - \$37,500,000 = \$4,000,000$ Then, $\$4,000,000 \div \$50,000,000 = .08 = 8\%$

13. An increase of 300% over x = 4x, so sales are 4 times as large.

14. Gross sales = $\$374,000 \div .85 = \$440,000$

15. $(1.05)(1.03) = 1.0815$, which represents an 8.15% increase in dollar sales volume

16. $\$525 - \$310 = \$215$; then, $\$215/\$525 = 40.9\%$

17. $30 will represent 55% of retail amount. Thus, retail will be $\$30 \div .55 = \$54.50$

18. $(\$40)(.60) - \$1 = \$23$

19. $(\$17,000)(1.34) = \$22,780$. Then, $\$22,780 - \$6000 = \$16,780$. Also, $\$17,000 - \$3,000 = \$14,000$. Finally, $(\$16,780 - \$14,000) \div \$14,000 \approx 19.9\%$

20. Let x = markup percent. Then, $x-40/x = .13$ Solving, $x = 46$

21. Cost = $(\$35)(.60) = \$21$

6 (#1)

22. Let x = retail price. Then, $1.20 = .60x. Solving, x = $2.00

23. $50 = 25% of retail, so retail = $200. Thus, cost = $200 - $50 = $150

24. Let x = overtime hours. Then, ($9.60)(40) + $14.40x = $470.40 Solving, x = 6. Total hours worked = 46

25. 5x - 3x - $12,000. So, x = $6000. Clarke's share = (3)($6000) = $18,000

TEST 2

DIRECTIONS: Each question or incomplete statement is followed by several suggested answers or completions. Select the one that BEST answers the question or completes the statement. *PRINT THE LETTER OF THE CORRECT ANSWER IN THE SPACE AT THE RIGHT.*

1. Assume that you require 77 dozen felt practice golf balls. Which of the following represents the LOWEST bid for these balls?

   A. 41¢ per half-dozen less a 3% discount
   B. 83¢ per dozen less a 7 1/2% discount
   C. 85¢ per dozen less a 10% discount
   D. $65.00 less a series discount of 3%, 2%

   1.____

2. Assume that you require 1,944 rulers, packed 12 to the box, 18 boxes to the carton. Which of the following represents the LOWEST bid for these rulers?

   A. 5 1/2¢ per ruler
   B. 6¢ for the first 750 rulers; 5 1/2¢ for the next 750 rulers; 4 1/2¢ for every ruler thereafter
   C. $11.85 per carton
   D. $110 less series discounts of 2%, 1%

   2.____

3. Assume that you require 20 cartons of colored raffia, cellophane wrapped in one lb. packages, 50 packages to the carton.
   Which of the following represents the LOWEST bid for the raffia?

   A. 8¢ per lb.; 15¢ per carton packing charge; 20¢ per carton delivery charge
   B. 9¢ per lb. less a 3% discount
   C. 10¢ per lb. for the first 150 lbs.; 9¢ per lb. for the next 200 lbs.; 80 for each lb. thereafter
   D. $83.50 less a 4 1/2% discount

   3.____

4. Assume that you require 50 yards of table felt, 48" wide, and 12 yards of table felt, 72" wide.
   Which of the following represents the LOWEST bid for this felt?

   A. 32¢ per yard (48" wide), 40¢ per yard (72" wide)
   B. 34¢ per yard (48" wide), 43¢ per yard (72" wide); series discounts of 5%, 3%
   C. 360 per yard (48" wide), 41¢ per yard (72" wide); 8% discount, packing charge 75¢
   D. $23.00 for the order, 9% discount, packing charge 50¢

   4.____

5. If the cost of 3 erasers is 5¢, the cost of 2 1/2 dozen erasers is

   A. 18¢   B. 37 1/2¢   C. 50¢   D. 31 1/2¢

   5.____

6. A circle graph of a budget shows the expenditure of 26.2% for housing, 28.4% for food, 12% for clothing, 12.7% for taxes, and the balance for miscellaneous items.
   The percent for miscellaneous items is

   A. 31.5   B. 79.3   C. 20.7   D. 68.5

   6.____

7. The cost of a broadloom rug measuring 4 feet by 6 feet, at $6.30 per square yard, is   7._____

   A. $16.80   B. $50.40   C. $37.60   D. $21.00

8. The number of tiles each measuring 2 inches by 3 inches needed for a wall 3 feet high   8._____
   and 5 feet long is

   A. 180   B. 30   C. 360   D. 60

9. Assume that you require 4 tons of fertilizer. The fertilizer is packed in 100 pound bags.   9._____
   Which of the following represents the LOWEST bid for the fertilizer?

   A. 6¢ per pound
   B. $5.50 per bag
   C. $7.00 for each of the first 30 bags; $5.00 for each bag thereafter
   D. $500.00 less 3 1/2% discount

10. Assume pencils are packed 5 gross to the case. A buyer requires 3,800 pencils each for   10._____
    three departments and 2,700 pencils for another department. Assume that the vendor
    will ship unbroken cases only directly to each department.
    How many cases should he buy?

    A. 21   B. 22   C. 48   D. 49

11. Assume that a buyer had to purchase 40,000 lbs. of salt. Which one of the following bids   11._____
    should he accept, assuming quality, service, and delivery terms are all the same?

    A. 1¢ per pound, 2%-30 days
    B. 99¢ per 100 lbs., 1%-30 days
    C. $19 per ton, 1%-30 days
    D. $18 per ton, net-30 days

12. Which one of the following four bids represents the BEST value, assuming delivery costs   12._____
    amount to $100?

    A. $1,000 f.o.b. buyer, less 2%-10 days
    B. $900 f.o.b. seller, less 2%-10 days
    C. $975 delivered, net cash 30 days
    D. $990 f.o.b. buyer, less 1%-10 days

13. Suppose that four suppliers make the following offers to sell 2,000 units of a particular   13._____
    commodity.
    Which one is the MOST advan12tageous proposal?

    A. $10 list, less 40% and 5%
    B. $5 cost, plus 20% to cover overhead and profit
    C. $10 list, less 20% and 20%
    D. $5 cost, plus 10% overhead and 10% for profit

14. Suppose that you purchase 100 units of an item at a list of $1 per unit less 40% and   14._____
    10%, and less 2% if paid within 10 days.
    If payment is made within the 10-day limit, the amount of the payment should be

    A. $52.92   B. $54.00   C. $58.80   D. $60.00

15. Assume that the 1987 cost of living factor was 100 and that a certain product was selling that year for $5 per unit. Assume further that at the present time the cost of living factor is 150.
If the selling price of the product increased 10% more than the cost of living during this period, at the present time the product would be selling for ____ per unit.

   A. $8.25   B. $10.50   C. $16.50   D. $7.75

16. A certain food is sold in 4 ounce cans at 10 for $1.00 and in 1 pound cans at 3 for $1.00. The savings in price per ounce by purchasing the food in the larger can is ____ cents/ounce.

   A. .53   B. .35   C. .42   D. .68

17. After an article is discounted at 25%, it sells for $375. The ORIGINAL price of the article was

   A. $93.75   B. $350   C. $375   D. $500

18. Assume that you require 1,440 pencils, packed 12 to the box, 24 boxes to the carton. Which of the following represents the LOWEST bid for these pencils?

   A. 2¢ per pencil
   B. $6.50 per carton
   C. 27¢ per box less a 4% discount
   D. $40 less a 3% discount

19. If erasers cost 8¢ each for the first 250, 7¢ each for the next 250, and 5¢ for every eraser thereafter, how many erasers may be purchased for $50?

   A. 600   B. 750   C. 850   D. 1,000

20. Assume that a buyer saves $14 on the purchase of an item that is discounted at 25%. The amount of money that the buyer must pay for the item is

   A. $42   B. $52   C. $54   D. $56

Questions 21-24.

DIRECTIONS: Questions 21 through 24 are to be answered on the basis of the following method of obtaining a reorder point: multiply the monthly rate of consumption by the lead time (in months) and add the minimum balance.

21. If the lead time is one-half month, the minimum balance is 6 units, and the monthly rate of consumption is 4 units, then the reorder point is ___ units.

   A. 4   B. 6   C. 8   D. 12

22. If the reorder point is 25 units, the lead time is 3 months, and the minimum balance is 10 units, then the average monthly rate of consumption is _____ units.

   A. 3   B. 5   C. 6   D. 10

23. If the reorder point is 400 units, the lead time is 2 months, and the monthly rate of consumption is 150 units, then the minimum balance is _____ units.

   A. 50   B. 100   C. 150   D. 200

24. If the reorder point is 75 units, the monthly rate of consumption is 60 units, and the minimum balance is 45 units, then the lead time is _____ month(s).

   A. 1/2   B. 1   C. 2   D. 4

25. A purchasing office has 4,992 special requisitions to be processed. Working alone, Buyer A could process these in 30 days; working alone, Buyer B could process these in 40 days; working alone, Buyer C could process these in 60 days.
   The LEAST number of days in which Buyers A, B, and C working together can process these 4,992 special requisitions is APPROXIMATELY _____ days.

   A. 14   B. 20   C. 34   D. 45

KEY (CORRECT ANSWERS)

1. C
2. B
3. D
4. B
5. C
6. C
7. A
8. C
9. B
10. B

11. D
12. C
13. A
14. A
15. A
16. C
17. D
18. A
19. B
20. A

21. C
22. B
23. B
24. A
25. A

SOLUTIONS TO PROBLEMS

1. Bid A = (.82)(77)(.97) ≈ $61.25;
    Bid B = (.83)(77)(.925) ≈ $59.12
    Bid C = (.85)(77)(.90) ≈ $58.91;
    Bid D = ($65.00)(.97)(.98) ≈ $61.79 Thus, Bid C is lowest.

2. Bid A = (.055)(1944) = $106.92;
    Bid B = (.06)(750)+(.055)(750) + (.045)(444) = $106.23;
    Bid C = ($11.85)(9) = $106.65;
    Bid D = ($110)(.98)(.99) ≈ $106.72. Thus, Bid B is lowest.

3. Bid A = (.08)(1000) + (.15)(20) + (.20)(20) = $87.00
    Bid B = (.09)(1000)(.97) = $87.30
    Bid C = (.10)(150) + (.09)(200) + (.08)(650) = $85.00
    Bid D = ($83.50)(.955) ≈ $79.74
    Thus, Bid D is lowest.

4. Bid A = (.32)(50)+(.40)(12) = $20.80
    Bid B = (.34)(50)+(.43)(12) = $22.16; so ($22.16)(.95)(.97) ≈ $20.42
    Bid C = (.36)(50)+(.41)(12) = $22.92; so ($22.92)(.92)+.75 ≈ $21.84
    Bid D = ($23.00)(.91)+.50 = $21.43
    Bid B is lowest.

5. (2 1/2)(12) = 30 erasers, which will cost (.05)(10) = 50¢

6. 100 - 26.2 - 28.4 - 12 - 12.7 = 20.7% for miscellaneous items

7. 24 ÷ 9 = 2 2/3 sq.yds. Then, ($6.30)(2 2/3) = $16.80

8. 3' 2" = 18; 5' 3" = 20. Thus, (18)(20) = 360 tiles

9. Bid A = (.06)(8000) = $480
    Bid B = ($5.50)(80) = $440
    Bid C = ($7.00)(30)+($5.00)(50) = $460 Bid D - ($500)(.965) = $482.50 Thus,
    Bid B is lowest.

10. 5 gross = 5(144) = 720; 3800 will be 6 unbroken cases x 3 = 18
                                     2700 will be 4 unbroken cases   = 4
                                                                             22

11. Bid A = (.01)(40,000)(.98) = $392.00
    Bid B = (.99)(400)(.99) = $392.04
    Bid C = ($19)(20)(.99) = $376.20
    Bid D = ($18)(20) = $360.00
    Bid D is lowest.

12. A. 1,000 - 2% = 980
    B. 900 + 100 - 2% = 980

C. 975
D. 990 - 9.90 = 980.10
C is best value

13. Proposal A: ($10)(.60)(.95) = $5.70
    Proposal B: $5 + ($5)(.20) = $6.00
    Proposal C: ($10) (.80)(.80) = $6.40
    Proposal D: $5 + (.20)($5) = $6.00
    Proposal A is lowest.

14. Payment = ($100)(.60)(.90)(.98) = $52.92

15. Present cost = ($5)(1.50)(1.10) = $8.25

16. 40 ounces for $1.00 in smaller cans means 2.5 cents per ounce. For the larger cans, (3)(16) = 48 ounces for $1.00, which means $2.08\overline{3}$ cents per ounce. The savings is approximately .42 cents per ounce.

17. Original price = $375 ÷ .75 = $500

18. Bid A = (1440)(.02) = $28.80
    Bid B = (1440 ÷ 288)($6.50) = $32.50
    Bid C = [(144 ÷ 12)(.27)] [.96] = $31.10
    Bid D = ($40)(.97) = $38.80
    Bid A is lowest.

19. 250 erasers cost (250)(.08) = $20
    500 erasers cost $20 + (250)(.07) = $37.50
    The number of additional erasers = ($50 - $37.50) ÷ .05 = 250
    Total number of erasers = 750

20. $14 ÷ .25 = $56. Then, $56 - $14 = $42

21. (4)(.5) +6 = 8 units

22. Let x = monthly rate. Then, (x)(3) + 10 = 25. Solving, x = 5 units

23. Let x = minimum balance. (150)(2) + x = 400. Solving, x = 100 units

24. Let x = lead time. (60)(x) + 45 = 75. Solving, x = 1/2 month

25. Buyer A does 4992 ÷ 30 ≈ 166 per day
    Buyer B does 4992 ÷ 40 ≈ 125 per day
    Buyer C does 4992 ÷ 60 ≈ 83 per day
    Working together, approximately 374 requisitions are done per day. Finally, 4992 ÷ 374 ≈ 13, closest to 14 in selections.

INTERPRETING STATISTICAL DATA
GRAPHS, CHARTS AND TABLES
TEST 1

DIRECTIONS: Study the following graphs, charts and/or tables. Base your answers to the questions that follow SOLELY on the information contained therein. *PRINT THE LETTER OF THE CORRECT ANSWER IN THE SPACE AT THE RIGHT.*

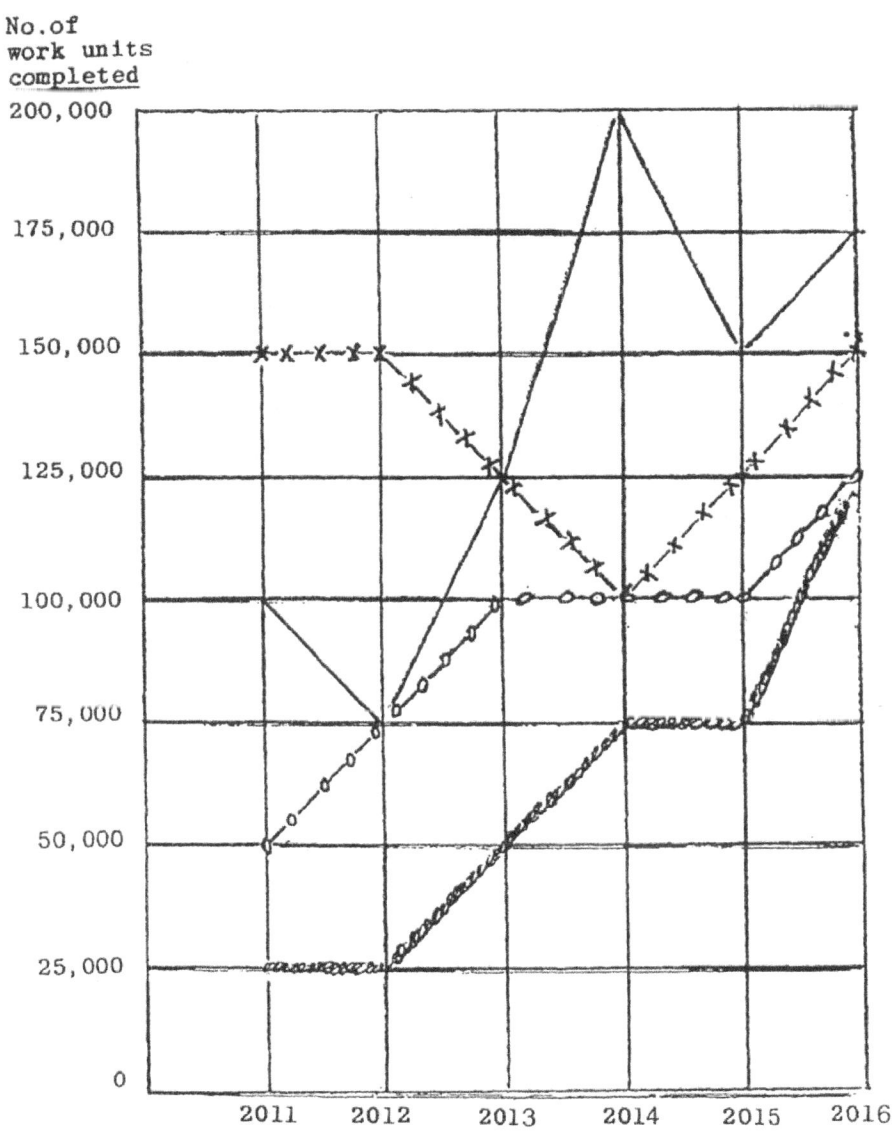

Units of each type of work completed by a public agency from 2011 to 2016.

```
Letters Written    _____
Documents Filed    ___X___X___X___X___
Applications Processed ___O___O___O___O
Inspections Made   ooooooooooooooooooo
```

1. The year for which the number of units of one type of work completed was *less* than it was for the previous year while the number of each of the other types of work completed was *more* than it was for the previous year was

   A. 2012   B. 2013   C. 2014   D. 2015

2. The number of letters written EXCEEDED the number of applications processed by the *same* amount in

   A. two of the years   B. three of the years
   C. four of the years D. five of the years

3. The YEAR in which the number of each type of work completed was *greater* than in the preceding year was

   A. 2013   B. 2014   C. 2015   D. 2016

4. The number of applications processed and the number of documents filed were the SAME in

   A. 2012   B. 2013   C. 2014   D. 2015

5. The *total number* of units of work completed by the agency

   A. increased in each year after 2011
   B. decreased from the prior year in two of the years after 2011
   C. was the same in two successive years from 2011 to 2016
   D. was less in 2011 than in any of the following years

6. For the year in which the number of letters written was twice as high as it was in 2011, the number of documents FILED was

   A. the same as it was in 2011
   B. two-thirds of what it was in 2011
   C. five-sixths of what it was in 2011
   D. one and one-half times what it was in 2011

7. The *variable* which was the MOST stable during the period 2011 through 2016 was

   A. Inspections Made   B. Letters Written
   C. Documents Filed   D. Applications Processed

KEY (CORRECT ANSWERS)

1. B   5. C
2. B   6. B
3. D   7. D
4. C

TEST 2

Questions 1-8.

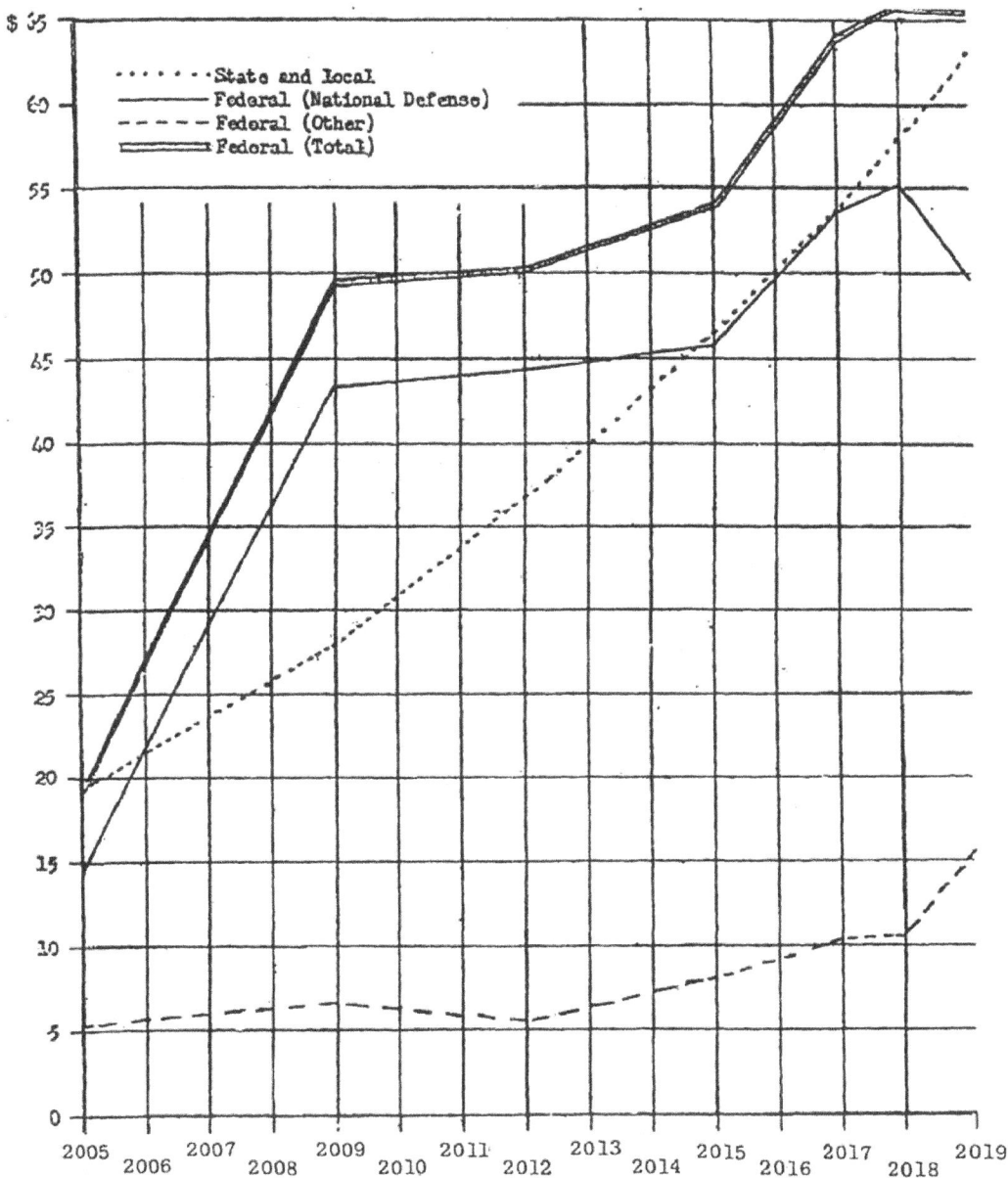

1. Purchases by the Federal government for non-defense purposes, and purchases by State and local governments comprised the smallest proportion of the total government purchases of goods and services for all purposes in which of the following years?

   A. 2005 B. 2009 C. 2012 D. 2015

1.____

2. Which one of the following MOST closely approximates the percentage increase in State and local purchases of goods and services in 2019 as compared with 2005?   2._____

   A. 110%   B. 150%   C. 220%   D. 350%

3. Total government purchases of goods and services in 2019 was MOST NEARLY _____ billion dollars.   3._____

   A. 80   B. 110   C. 128   D. 144

4. In 2015, purchases made by State and local governments   4._____

   A. exceeded Federal government total purchases
   B. exceeded purchases made by them in 2009 by more than 50%
   C. increased less than 10% over 2012
   D. were less than 50% of purchases made by them in 2018

5. Purchases of goods and services for national defense in 2009 by the Federal government was, MOST NEARLY,   5._____

   A. 15% less than the total spent by Federal, State and local governments for all purposes in 2005
   B. 50% of the total spent by Federal, State and local governments for all purposes in 2012
   C. four times the amount spent in 2005 for national defense
   D. ten times the amount spent in 2009 by the Federal government for purposes other than national defense

6. In which one of the following years did State and local purchases of goods and services comprise the GREATEST proportion of the total spent by all government jurisdictions?   6._____

   A. 2005   B. 2009   C. 2012   D. 2017

7. The dollar increase in purchases of goods and services was LEAST for which one of the following?   7._____

   A. State and local governments between 2005 and 2009
   B. State and local governments between 2012 and 2015
   C. Total Federal government between 2015 and 2017
   D. Federal government other than national defense between 2015 and 2018

8. The rate of increase in Federal purchases of goods and services for national defense was GREATEST between which of the following periods?   8._____

   A. From 2009 to 2012   B. From 2012 to 2015
   C. From 2015 to 2017   D. From 2017 to 2019

KEY (CORRECT ANSWERS)

1. B   5. B
2. C   6. A
3. C   7. D
4. B   8. C

TEST 3

Questions 1-10.

DIRECTIONS: Questions 1-10 are to be answered SOLELY on the basis of the following table showing the amounts purchased by various purchasing units during 2015.

DOLLAR VOLUME PURCHASED BY EACH PURCHASING UNIT DURING EACH QUARTER OF 2015
(Figures Shown Represent Thousands of Dollars)

Purchasing Unit	First Quarter	Second Quarter	Third Quarter	Fourth Quarter
A	578	924	698	312
B	1,426	1,972	1,586	1,704
C	366	494	430	716
D	1,238	1,708	1,884	1,546
E	730	742	818	774
F	948	1,118	1,256	788

1. The TOTAL dollar volume purchased by *all* of the purchasing units during 2015 approximated, *most nearly,*

   A. $2,000,000   B. $4,000,000   C. $20,000,000   D. $40,000,000

2. During which quarter was the GREATEST total dollar amount of purchases made?

   A. First   B. Second   C. Third   D. Fourth

3. Assume that the dollar volume purchased by Unit F during 2015 exceeded the dollar volume purchased by Unit F during 2014 was 50%. Then the dollar volume purchased by Unit F during 2014 was

   A. $2,055,000   B. $2,550,000   C. $2,740,000   D. $6,165,000

4. Which *one* of the following purchasing units showed the SHARPEST decrease in the amount purchased during the *fourth* quarter as compared with the *third* quarter? Unit

   A. A   B. B   C. D   D. E

5. Comparing the dollar volume purchased in the *second* quarter with the dollar volume purchased in the *third* quarter, the *decrease* in the dollar volume during the third quarter was PRIMARILY due to the decrease in the dollar volume purchased by Units

   A. A and B   B. C and D   C. C and E   D. C and F

6. Of the following, the unit which had the LARGEST number of dollars of increased purchases from any one quarter to the next following quarter was Unit

   A. A   B. B   C. C   D. D

7. Of the following, the unit with the LARGEST dollar volume of purchases during the *second half* of 2015 was Unit

   A. A   B. B   C. D   D. F

2 (#3)

8. Which one of the following *most closely* approximates the percentage which Unit B's total 2015 purchases represents of the total 2015 purchases of all units, including Unit B?　　8.____

   A. 10%　　B. 15%　　C. 25%　　D. 45%

9. Assume that research showed that each ten thousand dollars ($10,000) of purchases by Unit D during 2015 required an average of thirteen (13) man-hours of buyers' staff time. On that basis, which *one* of the following *most closely* approximates the NUMBER OF MAN-HOURS of buyers' staff time required by Unit D during 2015? _____ man-hours.　　9.____

   A. 1,800　　B. 8,000　　C. 68,000　　D. 78,000

10. Assume that research showed that each ten thousand dollars ($10,000) of purchases by Unit C during 2015 required an average of ten (10) man-hours of buyers' staff time. This research also showed that during 2015 the average man-hours of buyers' staff time per ten thousand dollars of purchases required by Unit C exceeded by 25% the average man-hours of buyers' staff time per ten thousand dollars of purchases required by Unit E. On that basis, which *one* of the following *most closely* approximates the NUMBER OF BUYER'S STAFF MAN-HOURS required by Unit E during 2015? _____ man-hours.　　10.____

    A. 2,200　　B. 2,400　　C. 3,000　　D. 3,700

KEY (CORRECT ANSWERS)

1. C
2. B
3. C
4. A
5. A

6. B
7. C
8. C
9. B
10. B

TEST 4

Questions 1-6.

DIRECTIONS: Questions 1 to 6 are to be answered SOLELY on the basis of the following table and graph and the accompanying notes.

CONSUMER PROTECTION DIVISION-METROPOLITAN CITY
Number and Kinds of Violations (2017-2019)

NATURE OF VIOLATION	2017 District						2018 District						2019 District					
	A	B	C	D	E	Total	A	B	C	D	E	Total	A	B	C	D	E	Total
Scales	27	31	42	16	12	128	18	34	36	15	19	122	20	28	31	12	10	101
Gasoline sales	12	9	17	6	3	47	9	4	19			32	6	5	16	3	6	36
Illegal meat coloring	9	8	13	4		34	10	12	21	9	2	54	8	6	5	2	1	22
Fat content-chopped meat	21	19	40	7	1	88	20	17	31	3	3	74	16	12	18	4	3	53
Checkout counter errors	12	9	10	2		33	12	8	21			41	16	21	9	2	2	50
Fuel oil sales	6	5	4		16	31			2		6	8	5	6	6		18	35
Fraudulent labels	18	29	39	14	14	114	21	36	31	12	18	118	12	25	19	15	25	96
TOTALS	105	110	165	49	46	475	90	111	161	39	48	449	83	103	104	38	65	393

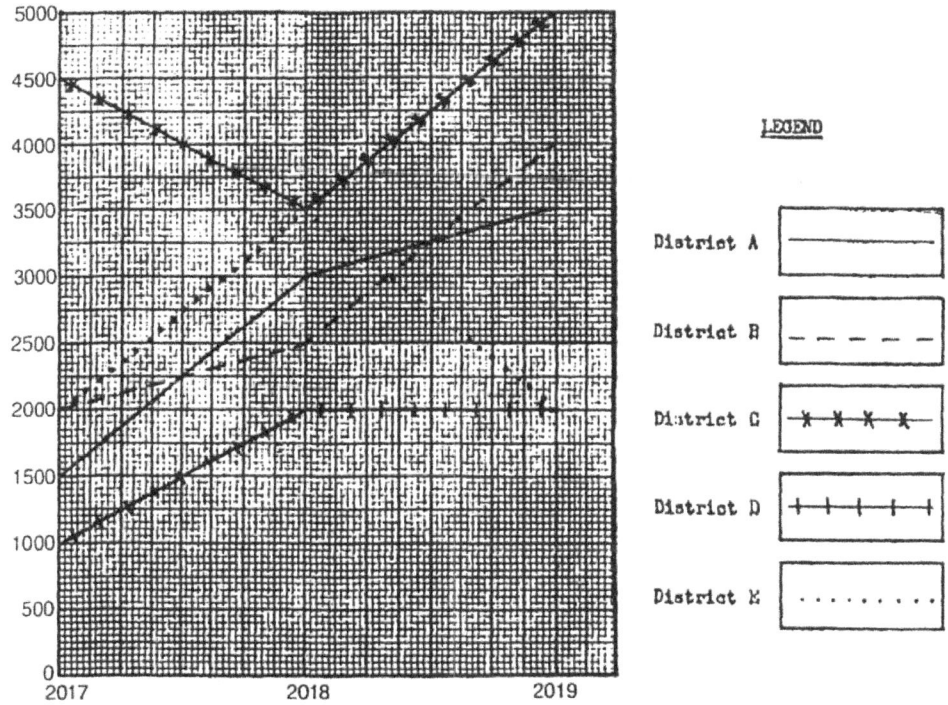

CONSUMER PROTECTION DIVISION-METROPOLITAN CITY
Number of Inspections Performed (2017 - 2019)

LEGEND

District A ————
District B — — — —
District C —×—×—×—
District D —+—+—+—
District E ·········

NOTES: The Consumer Protection Division of Metropolitan City is divided into five districts designated A, B, C, D and E.

2 (#4)

Number of establishments in each district:

District A - 26,000　　　District C - 27,000　　　District E - 12,000
District B - 30,000　　　District D - 15,000

Number of field inspectors assigned to each district in 2017 and 2018

District A - 20　　　District C - 25　　　District E - 11
District B - 24　　　District D - 21

At the beginning of 2019 there was a general reassignment of field inspectors and the staff of field inspectors was increased. This resulted in assignments of field inspectors as follows:

District A - 20　　　District C - 32　　　District E - 16
District B - 26　　　District D - 16

1. Of the following districts, the one in which the ratio of meat coloring violations to total number of violations in the district was GREATEST in 2018 is District 　　1.____

   A. A　　　B. B　　　C. C　　　D. D

2. In 2018, the number of violations uncovered per field inspector for the entire city was, *most nearly*, 　　2.____

   A. 3.9　　　B. 4.1　　　C. 4.4　　　D. 4.8

3. In 2017, the number of violations per 1,000 establishments in District C was, *most nearly*, 　　3.____

   A. 3.9　　　B. 6.1　　　C. 10.4　　　D. 16.5

4. The number of inspections performed by the Consumer Protection Division in 2018 was, most *nearly*, 　　4.____

   A. 449　　　B. 12,000　　　C. 13,500　　　D. 14,500

5. In 2017, the number of violations uncovered per 100 inspections for the entire city was, *most nearly*, 　　5.____

   A. .23　　　B. 3.2　　　C. 4.3　　　D. 48.0

6. If it had been decided at the beginning of 2019 to assign inspectors so that the ratio of the number of inspectors in each district to the total number of inspectors would be the same as the ratio of the number of establishments in the district to the total number of establishments in the city, the number of inspectors assigned to District A would have been 　　6.____

   A. 24　　　B. 25　　　C. 26　　　D. 27

KEY (CORRECT ANSWERS)

1. D　　4. D
2. C　　5. C
3. B　　6. C

TEST 5

Questions 1-4.

DIRECTIONS: Questions 1 to 4 are to be answered SOLELY on the basis of the following graph and the accompanying notes.

NOTES: The graph shows space allocation in three municipal food markets in a certain city. The five columns for each market represent the total amount of each market's space. The miscellaneous column accounts for all non-rental space allocated to shopping aisles, loading facilities, etc.

Assume that during 2019 there was no tenant turnover and that the amount of space rented and unrented remained constant.
The rental charges in 2019 for all types of business were as follows:
Jefferson Market - $10.00 per square foot
Jackson Market - $17.50 per square foot
Lincoln Market - $15.00 per square foot

2019 SPACE ALLOCATIONS IN THE JEFFERSON, JACKSON AND LINCOLN MUNICIPAL FOOD MARKETS
(According to Type of Business)

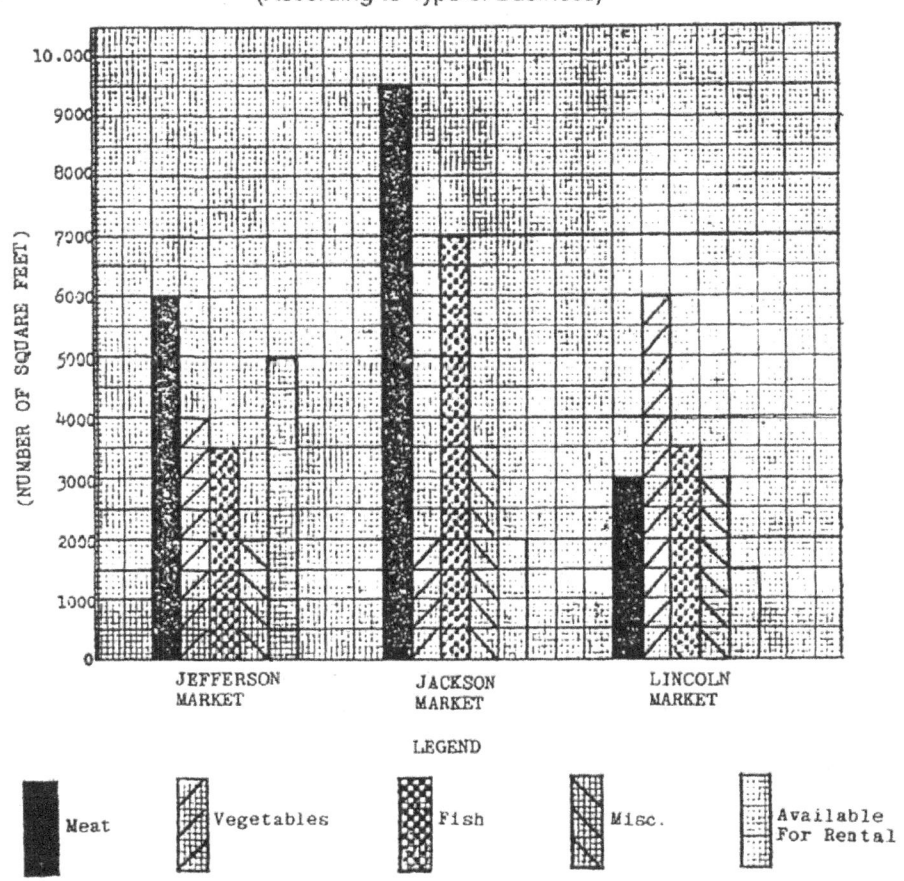

1. The percentage of overall space in the Lincoln Market leased to fish dealers in 2019 is, most nearly,

   A. 17% B. 19% C. 21% D. 23%

2. The total amount of space in all three municipal food markets devoted to the *meat business* EXCEEDED the amount of space in these markets devoted to the *fish business* by _____ square feet.

   A. 2,500 B. 4,500 C. 14,000 D. 18,500

3. If all of the space in the Lincoln Market available for rental in 2019 had been rented, the income received from this market would have INCREASED by

   A. 6% B. 12% C. 18% D. 24%

4. Approximately what percent of the 2019 rental income of the Jackson Market was derived from vegetable dealers?

   A. 8.3%
   B. 9.1%
   C. 10.8%
   D. a percent which cannot be determined from the data given

KEY (CORRECT ANSWERS)

1. C
2. B
3. B
4. C

TEST 6

Questions 1-5.

DIRECTIONS: Questions 1 to 5 involve calculation of annual grade averages for college students who have just completed their junior year. These averages are to be based on the following table showing the number of credit hours for each student during the year at each of the grade levels: A,B,C,D,and F. How these letter grades may be translated into numerical grades is indicated in the first column of the table.

Grade Value	Credit hours - Junior Year					
	King	Lewis	Martin	Norris	Ott	Perry
A = 95	12	12	9	15	6	3
B = 85	9	12	9	12	18	6
C = 75	6	6	9	3	3	21
D = 65	3	3	3	3	-	-
F = 0	-	-	3	-	-	-

NOTES: Calculating a grade average for an individual student is a 4-step process:
  I. Multiply each grade value by the number of credit hours for which the student received that grade.
  II. Add these multiplication products for each student.
  III. Add the student's total credit hours.
  IV. Divide the multiplication product total by the total number of credit hours.
  V. Round the result, if there is a decimal place, to the nearest whole number. A number ending in .5 would be rounded to the next higher number.

EXAMPLE: Using student King's grades as an example, his grade average can be calculated by going through the following four steps:

```
I.    95 x 12 = 1140        III.    12
      85 x  9 =  765                 9
      75 x  6 =  450                 6
      65 x  3 =  195                 3
       0 x  0 =    0                 0
II.        TOTAL = 2550              30  TOTAL credit hours
                            IV.    Divide 2550 by 30: 2550 / 30 = 85
```

King's grade average is 85.
Now answer questions 1 through 5 on the basis of the information given above.

1. The grade average of Lewis is
   A. 83   B. 84   C. 85   D. 86

2. The grade average of Martin is
   A. 72   B. 73   C. 74   D. 75

3. The grade average of Norris is
   A. 85   B. 86   C. 87   D. 88

4. Student Ott must attain a grade average of 90 in each of his years in college to be accepted into the graduate school of his choice. If, in summer school during his junior year, he takes two 3-credit courses and receives a grade of 95 in each one, his grade average for his junior year will then be, *most nearly*.

   A. 87   B. 88   C. 89   D. 90

5. If Perry takes an additional 3-credit course during the year and receives a grade of 95, his grade average will be increased to *approximately*

   A. 79   B. 80   C. 81   D. 82

KEY (CORRECT ANSWERS)

1. C
2. D
3. C
4. B
5. B

TEST 7

Questions 1-5.

DIRECTIONS: Questions 1 to 5 are to be answered SOLELY on the basis of the chart below which relates to the increase in taxes.

Increase In State and Local Taxes Per Person

	2017	2019	Percent Increase		2017	2019	Percent Increase
Delaware	$138	$372	170	Iowa	$180	$389	116
Maryland	161	411	156	Tennessee	118	252	114
New York	227	576	153	Arkansas	103	221	114
Nebraska	144	362	151	Wyoming	193	414	114
Kentucky	111	278	150	New Mexico	151	324	114
Rhode Island	153	379	148	Idaho	156	328	110
Virginia	128	314	145	Pennsylvania	162	340	109
Arizona	163	387	135	South Dakota	169	353	108
Indiana	141	334	137	Illinois	179	373	108
New Jersey	173	406	135	South Carolina	108	225	108
Wisconsin	187	439	135	Maine	149	308	106
California	232	540	133	Ohio	149	306	105
Michigan	184	428	132	Colorado	189	386	104
Missouri	132	301	128	Nevada	232	466	101
North Carolina	115	259	125	Connecticut	196	392	100
Vermont	173	384	123	Kansas	173	346	100
Minnesota	183	406	122	Texas	139	276	99
West Virginia	119	263	120	Utah	166	327	98
Massachusetts	206	453	119	New Hampshire	152	299	97
Alabama	103	224	118	North Dakota	176	338	92
Washington	189	410	117	Oregon	204	387	90
Florida	153	330	116	Oklahoma	152	287	89
Georgia	125	270	116	Louisiana	160	298	86
Mississippi	112	242	116	Montana	189	351	86

1. The dollar increase per person in taxes between 2017-2019 was GREATEST in which state?

   A. New York B. California C. Wisconsin
   D. New Jersey E. Delaware

2. The state whose people paid the LOWEST amount per person in taxes in 2019 was

   A. Montana B. Mississippi C. Alabama
   D. Arkansas E. South Carolina

3. Which of the following states DOUBLED its taxes from 2017 to 2019?   3._____

    A. Kentucky   B. North Carolina   C. Kansas
    D. Texas   E. None of these

4. Which state had the SMALLEST $ increase in taxes from 2017 to 2019?   4._____

    A. Montana   B. Alabama   C. Arkansas
    D. Mississippi   E. South Carolina

5. In which of the following states was the per capita tax the GREATEST in 2017?   5._____

    A. Massachusetts   B. New York   C. Nevada
    D. Delaware   E. Oregon

KEY (CORRECT ANSWERS)

1. A
2. D
3. C
4. E
5. C

TEST 8

Questions 1-6.

DIRECTIONS: Questions 1 to 6 are to be answered SOLELY on the basis of the chart below which relates to the Distribution of Minority Groups by Pay Category.

TABLE 1-- DISTRIBUTION OF ALL MINORITY GROUPS COMBINED, BY PAY CATEGORY AS OF NOVEMBER 30, 2019 AND MAY 31, 2020

Pay System	November 2019		May 2020		Percent Change
	Number	Percent	Number	Percent	
All Pay Systems	500,508	100.0	501,871	100.0	0.3
General Schedule and Similar	181,725	36.3	186,170	37.1	2.4
Wage Systems	155,744	31.1	151,919	30.3	-2.5
Postal Field Service	158,945	31.8	159,211	31.7	0.2
All Other	4,094	0.8	4,571	0.9	11.7

1. From the table, what was the TOTAL of government workers in *all* pay systems in November 2019?

   A. 155,744   B. 181,725   C. 186,170
   D. 500,508   E. None of these

2. What was the percentage difference between Wage Systems and All Pay Systems in November 2019 and Postal Field Service and All Pay Systems in May 2020?

   A. .2%   B. .6%   C. 1.1%   D. 1.7%   E. 2.5%

3. How many more minority group members were employed by the Postal Field Service in May 2020 than in November 2019?

   A. .2%   B. 256   C. 266   D. 1256   E. 1266

4. In which of the pay systems did the percentage of minority workers decline?

   A. General Schedule and Similar   B. Wage Systems
   C. Postal Field Service   D. All Other
   E. None of these

5. In which system was the percentage gain of minority members from 2019 to 2020 the greatest?

   A. General Schedule and similar   B. Wage Systems
   C. Postal Field Service   D. All Other systems
   E. One cannot tell from the information given

6. Which system reflects the GREATEST percentage increase from 2019 to 2020 to the total minority work force?

   A. General Schedule and similar   B. Wage systems
   C. Postal Field Service   D. All Other
   E. One cannot tell from the information given

KEY (CORRECT ANSWERS)

1. E
2. B
3. C
4. B
5. D
6. A

READING COMPREHENSION
UNDERSTANDING WRITTEN MATERIALS

COMMENTARY

The ability to read and understand written materials – texts, publications, newspapers, orders, directions, expositions – is a skill basic to a functioning democracy and to an efficient business or viable government.

That is why almost all examinations – for beginning, middle, and senior levels – test reading comprehension, directly or indirectly.

The reading test measures how well you understand what you read. This is how it is done: You read a passage followed by several statements. From these statements, you choose the *one* statement, or answer, that is *BEST* supported by, or *BEST* matches, what is said in the paragraph. *PRINT THE LETTER OF THE CORRECT ANSWER IN THE SPACE AT THE RIGHT.*

SAMPLE QUESTIONS

DIRECTIONS: Answer Questions 1 to 2 *only* according to the information given in the following passage.

When a fingerprint technician inks and takes rolled impressions of a subject's fingers, the degree of downward pressure the technician applies is important. The correct pressure may best be determined through experience and observation. It is quite important, however, that the subject be cautioned to relax and not help the fingerprint technician by also applying pressure, as this prevents the fingerprint technician from gaging the amount needed. A method which is helpful in getting the subject to relax his hand is to instruct him to look at some distant object and not to look at his hands.

1. According to this passage, the technician tries to relax the subject's hands by   1.____

    A. instructing him to let his hands hang loosely
    B. telling him that being fingerprinted is painless
    C. asking him to look at his hand instead of some distant object
    D. asking him to look at something other than his hand

2. The subject is asked *NOT* to press down on his fingers while being fingerprinted because   2.____

    A. the impressions taken become rolled
    B. the subject may apply too little downward pressure and spoil the impressions
    C. the technician cannot tell whether he is applying the right degree of pressure
    D. he doesn't have the experience to apply the exact amount of pressure

CORRECT ANSWERS
1. D
2. C

EXAMINATION SECTION
TEST 1

Questions 1-3.

DIRECTIONS: The following three questions relate to the information given in the paragraph below.

Thermostats should be tested in hot water for proper opening. A bucket should be filled with sufficient water to cover the thermostat and fitted with a thermometer suspended in the water so that the sensitive bulb portion does not rest directly on the bucket. The water is then heated on a stove. As the temperature of the water passes the 160-165° range, the thermostat should start to open and should be completely opened when the temperature has risen to 185-190°. Lifting the thermostat into the air should cause a pronounced closing action and the unit should be closed entirely within a short time.

1. The thermostat described above is a device which opens and closes with changes in the

    A. position   B. pressure   C. temperature   D. surroundings

2. According to the above paragraph, the closing action of the thermostat should be tested by

    A. working the thermostat back and forth
    B. permitting the water to cool gradually
    C. adding cold water to the bucket
    D. removing the thermostat from the bucket

3. The bulb of the thermometer should not rest directly on the bucket because

    A. the bucket gets hotter than the water
    B. the thermometer might be damaged in that position
    C. it is difficult to read the thermometer in that position
    D. the thermometer might interfere with operation of the thermostat

TEST 2

Questions 1-3.

DIRECTIONS: Questions 1 to 3 inclusive are to be answered in accordance with information given in the paragraph below.

All idle pumps should be turned daily by hand, and should be run under power at least once a week. Whenever repairs are made on a pump, a record should be kept so that it will be possible to judge the success with which the pump is performing its functions. If a pump fails to deliver liquid there may be an obstruction in the suction line, the pump's parts may be badly worn, or the packing defective.

1. According to the above paragraph, pumps   1.____

   A. in use should be turned by hand every day
   B. which are not in use should be run under power every day
   C. which are in daily use should be run under power several times a week
   D. which are not in use should be turned by hand every day

2. According to the above paragraph, the reason for keeping records of repairs made on   2.____
   pumps is to

   A. make certain that proper maintenance is being performed
   B. discover who is responsible for improper repairs
   C. rate the performance of the pumps
   D. know when to replace worn parts

3. The one of the following causes of pump failure which is NOT mentioned in the above   3.____
   paragraph is

   A. excessive suction lift   B. clogged lines
   C. bad packing   D. worn parts

TEST 3

Questions 1-5.

DIRECTIONS: Answer Questions 1 through 5 *SOLELY* on the basis of the information contained in the following passage.

Floors in warehouses, storerooms, and shipping rooms must be strong enough to stay level under heavy loads. Unevenness of floors may cause boxes of materials to topple and fall. Safe floor load capacities and maximum heights to which boxes may be stacked should be posted conspicuously so all can notice it. Where material in boxes, containers, or cartons of the same weight is regularly stored, it is good practice to paint a horizontal line on the wall indicating the maximum height to which the material may be piled. A qualified expert should determine floor load capacity from the building plans, the age and condition of the floor supports, the type of floor, and other related information.

Working aisles are those from which material is placed into and removed from storage. Working aisles are of two types: transportation aisles, running the length of the building, and cross aisles, running across the width of the building. Deciding on the number, width, and location of working aisles is important. While aisles are necessary and determine boundaries of storage areas, they reduce the space actually used for storage.

1. According to the passage above, how should safe floor load capacities be made known to employees? They should be

    A. given out to each employee
    B. given to supervisors only
    C. printed in large red letters
    D. posted so that they are easily seen

2. According to the passage above, floor load capacities should be determined by

    A. warehouse supervisors   B. the fire department
    C. qualified experts   D. machine operators

3. According to the above passage, transportation aisles

    A. run the length of the building
    B. run across the width of the building
    C. are wider than cross aisles
    D. are shorter than cross aisles

4. According to the above passage, working aisles tend to

    A. take away space that could be used for storage
    B. add to space that could be used for storage
    C. slow down incoming stock
    D. speed up outgoing stock

5. According to the passage above, unevenness of floors may cause

    A. overall warehouse deterioration
    B. piles of stock to fall
    C. materials to spoil
    D. many worker injuries

TEST 4

Questions 1-3.

DIRECTIONS: Questions 1 to 3 are to be answered SOLELY on the basis of the information contained in the following paragraph.

In a retail establishment, any overweight means a distinct loss to the merchant, and even an apparently inconsequential overweight on a single package or sale, when multiplied by the total number of transactions, could run into large figures. In addition to the use of reliable scales and weights, and their maintenance in proper condition, there must be proper supervision of the selling force. Such supervision is a difficult matter, particularly on the score of carelessness, as the depositing of extra amounts of material on the scale and failure to remove the same when it overbalances the scale may become a habit. In case of underweight, either in the weighing or by the use of fraudulent scales and weights, the seller soon will hear of it, but there is no reason why the amount weighed out should be in excess of what the customer pays for. Checking sales records against invoices and inventories can supply some indication of the tendency of the sales force to become careless in this field.

1. Of the following, the MOST valid implication of the above paragraph is that 1.____

   A. all overweights which occur in retail stores are in small amounts
   B. even-arm and uneven-arm balances and weights which are unreliable lead more often to underweights than to overweights
   C. overweights due to errors of salesclerks necessarily lead to large losses by a retailer
   D. supervision to prevent overweights is more important to a retailer than remedial measures after their occurrence

2. Of the following, the MOST valid implication of the above paragraph is that 2.____

   A. depositing of insufficient amounts of commodities on scales and failure to add to them may become a habit with salesclerks
   B. salesclerks should be trained in understanding and maintenance of scale mechanisms
   C. supervision of salesclerks to prevent careless habits in weighing must depend upon personal observation
   D. training and supervision of salesclerks in proper estimation of the amount asked for by the customer can eliminate errors of overweight

3. According to the above paragraph, the MOST accurate of the following statements is: 3.____

   A. For the most part, the ideas expressed in the paragraph do not apply to wholesale establishments.
   B. Inventories of commodities prepacked in the store are the only ones which can be used in checking losses due to overweight.
   C. Invoices which give the value and weight of merchandise received are useful in checking losses due to overweights.
   D. The principal value of inventories is to indicate losses due to overweights.

TEST 5

Questions 1-5.

DIRECTIONS: Read the information below carefully. Then answer Questions 1 to 5 SOLELY on the basis of this information.

TITANIC AIR COMPRESSOR

Valves: The compressors are equipped with Titanic plate valves which are automatic in operation. Valves are so constructed that an entire valve assembly can readily be removed from the head. The valves provide large port areas with short lift and are accurately guided to Insure positive seating.

Starting Unloader: Each compressor (or air end) is equipped with a centrifugal governor which is bolted directly to the compressor crank shaft. The governor actuates cylinder relief valves so as to relieve pressure from the cylinders during starting and stopping. The motor is never required to start the compressor tinder load.

Air Strainer: Each cylinder air inlet connection is fitted with a suitable combination air strainer and muffler.

Pistons: Pistons are light-weight castings, ribbed internally to secure strength, and are accurately turned and ground. Each piston is fitted with four (4) rings, two of which are oil control rings. Piston pins are hardened and tempered steel of the full floating type. Bronze bushings are used between piston pin and piston.

Connecting Rods: Connecting rods are of solid bronze designed for maximum strength, rigidity and wear. Crank pins are fitted with renewable steel bushings. Connecting rods are of the one-piece type, there being no bolts, nuts, or cotter pins which can come loose. With this type of construction, wear is reduced to a negligible amount, and adjustment of wrist pin and crank pin bearings is unnecessary.

Main Bearings: Main bearings are of the ball type and are securely held in position by spacers. This type of bearing entirely eliminates the necessity of frequent adjustment or attention. The crank shaft is always in perfect alignment.

Crank Shaft: The crank shaft is a one-piece heat-treated forging of best quality open-hearth steel, of rugged design and of sufficient size to transmit the motor power and any additional stresses which may occur in service. Each crank shaft is counter-balanced Cdynamically balanced) to reduce vibration to a minimum, and is accurately machined to properly receive the ball-bearing races, crank pin bushing, flexible coupling, and centrifugal governor. Suitable provision is made to insure proper lubrication of all crank shaft bearings and bushings with the minimum amount of attention.

Coupling: Compressor and motor shafts are connected through a Morse Chain Company all-metal enclosed flexible coupling. This coupling consists of two sprockets, one mounted on, and keyed to, each shaft; the sprockets are wrapped by a single Morse Chain, the entire assembly being enclosed in a split aluminum grease-packed cover.

1. The crank pin of the connecting rod is fitted with a renewable bushing made of   1.____

    A. solid bronze
    B. steel
    C. a light-weight casting
    D. ball bearings

2. When the connecting rod is of the one-piece type,   2.____

    A. the wrist pins require frequent adjustment
    B. the crank pins require frequent adjustment

C. the cotter pins frequently will come loose
D. wear is reduced to a negligible amount

3. The centrifugal governor is bolted *directly* to the

   A. compressor crank shaft
   B. main bearing
   C. piston pin
   D. muffler

   3.____

4. The *number* of oil control rings required for each piston is

   A. one
   B. two
   C. three
   D. four

   4.____

5. The compressor and motor shafts are connected through a flexible coupling. These couplings are

   A. keyed to the shafts
   B. brazed to the shafts
   C. soldered to the shafts
   D. press-fit to the shafts

   5.____

TEST 6

Questions 1-6.

DIRECTIONS: Answer Questions 1 to 6 *only* according to the information given in the paragraph below.

Perhaps the strongest argument the mass transit backer has is the advantage in efficiency that mass transit has over the automobile in the urban traffic picture. It has been estimated that given comparable location and construction conditions, the subway can carry four times as many passengers per hour and cost half as much to build as urban highways. Yet public apathy regarding the mass transportation movement in the 1960's resulted in the building of more roads. Planned to provide 42,000 miles of highways in the period from 1956-72, including 7500 miles within cities, the Federal Highway System project is now about two-thirds completed. The Highway Trust Fund supplies 90 percent of the cost of the System, with state and local sources putting up the rest of the money. By contrast, a municipality has had to put up the bulk of the cost of a rapid transit system. Although the System and its Trust Fund have come under attack in the past few years from environmentalists and groups opposed to the continued building of urban freeways – considered to be the most expensive, destructive, and inefficient segments of the System – a move by them to get the Trust Fund transformed into a general transportation fund at the expiration of the present program in 1972 seems to be headed nowhere.

1. Given similar building conditions and location, a city that builds a subway instead of a highway can expect to receive for each dollar spent

   A. half as much transport value
   B. twice as much transport value
   C. four times as much transport value
   D. eight times as much transport value

2. The general attitude of the public in the past ten years toward the mass transportation movement has been

   A. favorable   B. indifferent
   C. enthusiastic   D. unfriendly

3. The number of miles of highways still to be completed in the Federal Highway System project is, most nearly,

   A. 2,500   B. 5,000   C. 14,000   D. 28,000

4. What do certain groups who object to some features of the Federal Highway System program want to do with the Highway Trust Fund after 1972?

   A. Extend it in order to complete the project
   B. Change it so that the money can be used for all types of transportation
   C. End it even if the project is not completed
   D. Change it so that the money will be used only for urban freeways

5. *Which one* of the following statements is a *VALID* conclusion based on the facts in the above passage?

A. The advantage of greater efficiency is the only argument that supporters of the mass transportation movement can offer.
B. It was easier for cities to build roads rather than mass transit systems in the last 15 years because of the large financial contribution made by the Federal Government.
C. Mass transit systems cause as much congestion and air pollution in cities as automobiles.
D. In 1972, the Highway Trust Fund becomes a general transportation fund.

6. The *MAIN* idea or theme of the above passage is that the 6.____

    A. cost of the Federal Highway System is shared by the federal, state, and local governments
    B. public is against spending money for building mass transportation facilities in the cities
    C. cities would benefit more from expansion and improvement of their mass transit systems than from the building of more highways
    D. building of mass transportation facilities has been slowed by the Highway Trust Fund

TEST 7

Questions 1-5.

DIRECTIONS: Answer Questions 1 to 5 ONLY according to the information given in the paragraph below.

The use of role-playing as a training technique was developed during the past decade by social scientists, particularly psychologists, who have been active in training experiments. Originally, this technique was applied by clinical psychologists who discovered that a patient appears to gain understanding of an emotionally disturbing situation when encouraged to act out roles in that situation. As applied in government and business organizations, the purpose of role-playing is to aid employees to understand certain work problems involving interpersonal relations and to enable observers to evaluate various reactions to them. Thus, for example, on the problem of handling grievances, two individuals from the group might be selected to act out extemporaneously the parts of subordinate and supervisor. When this situation is enacted by various pairs among the class and the techniques and results are discussed, the members of the group are presumed to reach conclusions about the most effective means of handling similar situations. Often the use of role reversal, where participants take parts different from their actual work roles, assists individuals to gain more insight into other people's problems and viewpoints. Although role-playing can be a rewarding training device, the trainer must be aware of his responsibilities. If this technique is to be successful, thorough briefing of both actors and observers as to the situation in question, the participants' roles, and what to look for, is essential.

1. The role-playing technique was FIRST used for the purpose of

   A. measuring the effectiveness of training programs
   B. training supervisors in business organizations
   C. treating emotionally disturbed patients
   D. handling employee grievances

2. When role-playing is used in private business as a training device, the CHIEF aim is to

   A. develop better relations between supervisor and subordinate in the handling of grievances
   B. come up with a solution to a specific problem that has arisen
   C. determine the training needs of the group
   D. increase employee understanding of the human-relation factors in work situations

3. From the above passage, it is MOST reasonable to conclude that when role-playing is used, it is preferable to have the roles acted out by

   A. only one set of actors
   B. no more than two sets of actors
   C. several different sets of actors
   D. the trainer or trainers of the group

4. It can be *inferred* from the above passage that a limitation of role-play as a training method is that

   A. many work situations do not lend themselves to role-play
   B. employees are not experienced enough as actors to play the roles realistically
   C. only trainers who have psychological training can use it successfully
   D. participants who are observing and not acting do not benefit from it

5. To obtain *good* results from the use of role-play in training, a trainer should give participants

    A. a minimum of information about the situation so that they can act spontaneously
    B. scripts which illustrate the best method for handling the situation
    C. a complete explanation of the problem and the roles to be acted out
    D. a summary of work problems which involve interpersonal relations

5._____

KEY (CORRECT ANSWERS)

TEST 1	TEST 2	TEST 3	TEST 4
1. C	1. A	1. D	1. D
2. D	2. C	2. C	2. C
3. A	3. A	3. A	3. C
		4. A	
		5. B	

TEST 5	TEST 6	TEST 7
1. B	1. D	1. C
2. D	2. B	2. D
3. A	3. C	3. C
4. B	4. B	4. A
5. A	5. B	5. C
	6. C	

PREPARING WRITTEN MATERIAL

PARAGRAPH REARRANGEMENT
COMMENTARY

The sentences which follow are in scrambled order. You are to rearrange them in proper order and indicate the letter choice containing the correct answer at the space at the right.

Each group of sentences in this section is actually a paragraph presented in scrambled order. Each sentence in the group has a place in that paragraph; no sentence is to be left out. You are to read each group of sentences and decide upon the best order in which to put the sentences so as to form as well-organized paragraph.

The questions in this section measure the ability to solve a problem when all the facts relevant to its solution are not given.

More specifically, certain positions of responsibility and authority require the employee to discover connections between events sometimes, apparently, unrelated. In order to do this, the employee will find it necessary to correctly infer that unspecified events have probably occurred or are likely to occur. This ability becomes especially important when action must be taken on incomplete information.

Accordingly, these questions require competitors to choose among several suggested alternatives, each of which presents a different sequential arrangement of the events. Competitors must choose the MOST logical of the suggested sequences.

In order to do so, they may be required to draw on general knowledge to infer missing concepts or events that are essential to sequencing the given events. Competitors should be careful to infer only what is essential to the sequence. The plausibility of the wrong alternatives will always require the inclusion of unlikely events or of additional chains of events which are NOT essential to sequencing the given events.

It's very important to remember that you are looking for the best of the four possible choices, and that the best choice of all may not even be one of the answers you're given to choose from.

There is no one right way to solve these problems. Many people have found it helpful to first write out the order of the sentences, as they would have arranged them, on their scrap paper before looking at the possible answers. If their optimum answer is there, this can save them some time. If it isn't, this method can still give insight into solving the problem. Others find it most helpful to just go through each of the possible choices, contrasting each as they go along. You should use whatever method feels comfortable, and works, for you.

While most of these types of questions are not that difficult, we've added a higher percentage of the difficult type, just to give you more practice. Usually there are only one or two questions on this section that contain such subtle distinctions that you're unable to answer confidently, and you then may find yourself stuck deciding between two possible choices, neither of which you're sure about.

Preparing Written Material

EXAMINATION SECTION
TEST 1

DIRECTIONS: The following groups of sentences need to be arranged in an order that makes sense. Select the letter preceding the sequence that represents the best sentence order. *PRINT THE LETTER OF THE CORRECT ANSWER IN THE SPACE AT THE RIGHT.*

Question 1

1. The ostrich egg shell's legendary toughness makes it an excellent substitute for certain types of dishes or dinnerware, and in parts of Africa ostrich shells are cut and decorated for use as containers for water.
2. Since prehistoric times, people have used the enormous egg of the ostrich as a part of their diet, a practice which has required much patience and hard work-to hard-boil an ostrich egg takes about four hours.
3. Opening the egg's shell, which is rock hard and nearly an inch thick, requires heavy tools, such as a saw or chisel; from inside, a baby ostrich must use a hornlike projection on its beak as a miniature pick-axe to escape from the egg.
4. The offspring of all higher-order animals originate from single egg cells that are carried by mothers, and most of these eggs are relatively small, often microscopic.
5. The egg of the African ostrich, however, weighs a massive thirty pounds, making it the largest single cell on earth, and a common object of human curiosity and wonder.

The best order is

A. 5 4 1 2 3
B. 1 4 5 3 2
C. 4 2 3 5 1
D. 4 5 2 3 1

Question 2

1. Typically only a few feet high on the open sea, individual tsunami have been known to circle the entire globe two or three times if their progress is not interrupted, but are not usually dangerous until they approach the shallow water that surrounds land masses.
2. Some of the most terrifying and damaging hazards caused by earthquakes are tsunami, which were once called "tidal waves"— a poorly chosen name, since these waves have nothing to do with tides.
3. Then a wave, slowed by the sudden drag on the lower part of its moving water column, will pile upon itself, sometimes reaching a height of over 100 feet.
4. Tsunami (Japanese for "great harbor wave") are seismic waves that are caused by earthquakes near oceanic trenches, and once triggered, can travel up to 600 miles an hour on the open ocean.
5. A land-shoaling tsunami is capable of extraordinary destruction; some tsunami have deposited large boats miles inland, washed out two-foot-thick seawalls, and scattered locomotive trains over long distances.

The best order is

A. 4 1 3 2 5
B. 1 3 4 2 5
C. 5 1 3 2 4
D. 2 4 1 3 5

Question 3

1. Soon, by the 1940's, jazz was the most popular type of music among American intellectuals and college students.
2. In the early days of jazz, it was considered "lowdown" music, or music that was played only in rough, disreputable bars and taverns.
3. However, jazz didn't take long to develop from early ragtime melodies into more complex, sophisticated forms, such as Charlie Parker's "bebop" style of jazz.
4. After charismatic band leaders such as Duke Ellington and Count Basic brought jazz to a larger audience, and jazz continued to evolve into more complicated forms, white audiences began to accept and even to enjoy the new American art form.
5. Many white Americans, who then dictated the tastes of society, were wary of music that was played almost exclusively in black clubs in the poorer sections of cities and towns.

The best order is

A. 5 4 3 2 1
B. 2 5 3 4 1
C. 4 5 3 1 2
D. 1 2 4 3 5

Question 4

1. Then, hanging in a windless place, the magnetized end of the needle would always point to the south.
2. The needle could then be balanced on the rim of a cup, or the edge of a fingernail, but this balancing act was hard to maintain, and the needle often fell off.
3. Other needles would point to the north, and it was important for any traveler finding his way with a compass to remember which kind of magnetized needle he was carrying.
4. To make some of the earliest compasses in recorded history, ancient Chinese "magicians" would rub a needle with a piece of magnetized iron called a lodestone.
5. A more effective method of keeping the needle free to swing with its magnetic pull was to attach a strand of silk to the center of the needle with a tiny piece of wax.

The best order is

A. 4 2 5 1 3
B. 4 3 5 2 1
C. 4 5 2 1 3
D. 4 1 3 5 2

Question 5

1. The now-famous first mate of the *HMS Bounty*, Fletcher Christian, founded one of the world's most peculiar civilizations in 1790.
2. The men knew they had just committed a crime for which they could be hanged, so they set sail for Pitcairn, a remote, abandoned island in the far eastern region of the Polynesian archipelago, accompanied by twelve Polynesian women and six men.
3. In a mutiny that has become legendary, Christian and the others forced Captain Bligh into a lifeboat and set him adrift off the coast of Tonga in April of 1789.
4. In early 1790, the *Bounty* landed at Pitcairn Island, where the men lived out the rest of their lives and founded an isolated community which to this day includes direct descendants of Christian and the other crewmen.
5. The *Bounty*, commanded by Captain William Bligh, was in the middle of a global voyage, and Christian and his shipmates had come to the conclusion that Bligh was a reckless madman who would lead them to their deaths unless they took the ship from him.

The best order is

A. 4 5 3 2 1
B. 1 3 5 2 4
C. 1 5 3 2 4
D. 3 1 5 4 2

Question 6

1. But once the vines had been led to make orchids, the flowers had to be carefully hand-pollinated, because unpollinated orchids usually lasted less than a day, wilting and dropping off the vine before it had even become dark.
2. The Totonac farmers discovered that looping a vine back around once it reached a five-foot height on its host tree would cause the vine to flower.
3. Though they knew how to process the fruit pods and extract vanilla's flavoring agent, the Totonacs also knew that a wild vanilla vine did not produce abundant flowers or fruit.
4. Wild vines climbed along the trunks and canopies of trees, and this constant upward growth diverted most of the vine's energy to making leaves instead of the orchid flowers that, once pollinated, would produce the flavorful pods.
5. Hundreds of years before vanilla became a prized food flavoring in Europe and the Western World, the Totonac Indians of the Mexican Gulf Coast were skilled cultivators of the vanilla vine, whose fruit they literally worshipped as a goddess.

The best order is

A. 2 3 4 1 5
B. 2 4 3 1 5
C. 5 3 4 2 1
D. 3 4 1 2 5

Question 7

1. Once airborne, the spider is at the mercy of the air currents—usually the spider takes a brief journey, traveling close to the ground, but some have been found in air samples collected as high as 10,000 feet, or been reported landing on ships far out at sea.
2. Once a young spider has hatched, it must leave the environment into which it was born as quickly as possible, in order to avoid competing with its hundreds of brothers and sisters for food.
3. The silk rises into warm air currents, and as soon as the pull feels adequate the spider lets go and drifts up into the air, suspended from the silk strand in the same way that a person might parasail.
4. To help young spiders do this, many species have adapted a practice known as "aerial dispersal," or, in common speech, "ballooning."
5. A spider that wants to leave its surroundings quickly will climb to the top of a grass stem or twig, face into the wind, and aim its back end into the air, releasing a long stream of silk from the glands near the tip of its abdomen.

The best order is

A. 5 4 2 3 1
B. 5 2 4 1 3
C. 2 5 4 3 1
D. 2 4 5 3 1

Question 8

1. For about a year, Tycho worked at a castle in Prague with a scientist named Johannes Kepler, but their association was cut short by another argument that drove Kepler out of the castle, to later develop, on his own, the theory of planetary orbits.
2. Tycho found life without a nose embarrassing, so he made a new nose for himself out of silver, which reportedly remained glued to his face for the rest of his life.
3. Tycho Brahe, the 17th-century Danish astronomer, is today more famous for his odd and arrogant personality than for any contribution he has made to our knowledge of the stars and planets.
4. Early in his career, as a student at Rostock University, Tycho got into an argument with the another student about who was the better mathematician, and the two became so angry that the argument turned into a sword fight, during which Tycho's nose was sliced off.
5. Later in his life, Tycho's arrogance may have kept him from playing a part in one of the greatest astronomical discoveries in history: the elliptical orbits of the solar system's planets.

The best order is

A. 1 4 2 3 5
B. 4 2 3 5 1
C. 4 2 1 3 5
D. 3 4 2 5 1

Question 9

1. The processionaries are so used to this routine that if a person picks up the end of a silk line and brings it back to the origin—creating a closed circle—the caterpillars may travel around and around for days, sometimes starving ar freezing, without changing course.
2. Rather than relying on sight or sound, the other caterpillars, who are lined up end-to-end behind the leader, travel to and from their nests by walking on this silk line, and each will reinforce it by laying down its own marking line as it passes over.
3. In order to insure the safety of individuals, the processionary caterpillar nests in a tree with dozens of other caterpillars, and at night, when it is safest, they all leave together in search of food.
4. The processionary caterpillar of the European continent is a perfect illustration of how much some insect species rely on instinct in their daily routines.
5. As they leave their nests, the processionaries form a single-file line behind a leader who spins and lays out a silk line to mark the chosen path.

The best order is

A. 4 3 5 2 1
B. 3 5 4 2 1
C. 3 5 2 1 4
D. 4 5 3 1 2

Question 10

1. Often, the child is also given a handcrafted walker or push cart, to provide support for its first upright explorations.
2. In traditional Indian families, a child's first steps are celebrated as a ceremonial event, rooted in ancient myth.
3. These carts are often intricately designed to resemble the chariot of Krishna, an important figure in Indian mythology.
4. The sound of these anklet bells is intended to mimic the footsteps of the legendary child Rama, who is celebrated in devotional songs throughout India.
5. When the child's parents see that the child is ready to begin walking, they will fit it with specially designed ankle bracelets, adorned with gently ringing bells.

The best order is

A. 2 3 4 1 5
B. 2 5 3 1 4
C. 5 4 1 3 2
D. 5 3 2 1 4

Question 11   11._____

1. The settlers planted Osage orange all across Middle America, and today long lines and rectangles of Osage orange trees can still be seen on the prairies, running along the former boundaries of farms that no longer exist.
2. After trying sod walls and water-filled ditches with no success, American farmers began to look for a plant that was adaptable to prairie weather, and that could be trimmed into a hedge that was "pig-tight, horse-high, and bull-strong."
3. The tree, so named because it bore a large (but inedible) fruit the size of an orange, was among the sturdiest and hardiest of American trees, and was prized among Native Americans for the strength and flexibility of bows which were made from its wood.
4. The first people to practice agriculture on the American flatlands were faced with an important problem: what would they use to fence their land in a place that was almost entirely without trees or rocks?
5. Finally, an Illinois farmer brought the settlers a tree that was native to the land between the Red and Arkansas rivers, a tree called the Osage orange.

The best order is

A. 2 1 5 3 4
B. 1 2 3 4 5
C. 4 2 5 3 1
D. 4 2 1 3 5

Question 12   12._____

1. After about ten minutes of such spirited and complicated activity, the head dancer is free to make up his or her own movements while maintaining the interest of the New Year's crowd.
2. The dancer will then perform a series of leg kicks, while at the same time operating the lion's mouth with his own hand and moving the ears and eyes by means of a string which is attached to the dancer's own mouth.
3. The most difficult role of this dance belongs to the one who controls the lion's head; this person must lead all the other "parts" of the lion through the choreographed segments of the dance.
4. The head dancer begins with a complex series of steps, alternately stepping forward with the head raised, and then retreating a few steps while lowering the head, a movement that is intended to create the impression that the lion is keeping a watchful eye for anything evil.
5. When performing a traditional Chinese New Year's lion dance, several performers must fit themselves inside a large lion costume and work together to enact different parts of the dance.

The best order is

A. 5 3 4 2 1
B. 3 4 2 5 1
C. 3 1 5 4 2
D. 4 2 3 5 1

Question 13

1. For many years the shell of the chambered nautilus was treasured in Europe for its beauty and intricacy, but collectors were unaware that they were in possession of the structure that marked a "missing link" in the evolution of marine mollusks.
2. The nautilus, however, evolved a series of enclosed chambers in its shell, and invented a new use for the structure: the shell began to serve as a buoyancy device.
3. Equipped with this new flotation device, the nautilus did not need the single, muscular foot of its predecessors, but instead developed flaps, tentacles, and a gentle form of jet propulsion that transformed it into the first mollusk able to take command of its own destiny and explore a three-dimensional world.
4. By pumping and adjusting air pressure into the chambers, the nautilus could spend the day resting on the bottom, and then rise toward the surface at night in search of food.
5. The nautilus shell looks like a large snail shell, similar to those of its ancestors, who used their shells as protective coverings while they were anchored to the sea floor.

The best order is

A. 5 2 4 1 3
B. 5 1 2 3 4
C. 1 2 5 3 4
D. 1 5 2 4 3

Question 14

1. While France and England battled for control of the region, the Acadiens prospered on the fertile farmland, which was finally secured by England in 1713.
2. Early in the 17th century, settlers from western France founded a colony called Acadie in what is now the Canadian province of Nova Scotia.
3. At this time, English officials feared the presence of spies among the Acadiens who might be loyal to their French homeland, and the Acadiens were deported to spots along the Atlantic and Caribbean shores of America.
4. The French settlers remained on this land, under English rule, for around forty years, until the beginning of the French and Indian War, another conflict between France and England.
5. As the Acadien refugees drifted toward a final home in southern Louisiana, neighbors shortened their name to "Cadien," and finally "Cajun," the name which the descendants of early Acadiens still call themselves.

The best order is

A. 1 4 2 3 5
B. 2 1 3 5 4
C. 2 1 4 3 5
D. 5 2 3 4 1

Question 15

1. Traditional households in the Eastern and Western regions of Africa serve two meals a day-one at around noon, and the other in the evening.
2. The starch is then used in the way that Americans might use a spoon, to scoop up a portion of the main dish on the person's plate.
3. The reason for the starch's inclusion in every meal has to do with taste as well as nutrition; African food can be very spicy, and the starch is known to cool the burning effect of the main dish.
4. When serving these meals, the main dish is usually served on individual plates, and the starch is served on a communal plate, from which diners break off a piece of bread or scoop rice or fufu in their fingers.
5. The typical meals usually consist of a thick stew or soup as the main course, and an accompanying starch–either bread, rice, *or fufu, a* starchy grain paste similar in consistency to mashed potatoes.

The best order is

A. 5 2 3 4 1
B. 5 1 4 3 2
C. 1 4 5 3 2
D. 1 5 4 2 3

Question 16

1. In the early days of the American Midwest, Indiana settlers sometimes came together to hold an event called an apple peeling, where neighboring settlers gathered at the homestead of a host family to help prepare the hosts' apple crop for cooking, canning, and making apple butter.
2. At the beginning of the event, each peeler sat down in front of a ten- or twenty-gallon stone jar and was given a crock of apples and a paring knife.
3. Once a peeler had finished with a crock, another was placed next to him; if the peeler was an unmarried man, he kept a strict count of the number of apples he had peeled, because the winner was allowed to kiss the girl of his choice.
4. The peeling usually ended by 9:30 in the evening, when the neighbors gathered in the host family's parlor for a dance social.
5. The apples were peeled, cored, and quartered, and then placed into the jar.

The best order is

A. 1 5 3 4 2
B. 2 5 3 4 1
C. 1 2 5 3 4
D. 2 1 5 4 3

Question 17

1. If your pet turtle is a land turtle and is native to temperate climates, it will stop eating some time in October, which should be your cue to prepare the turtle for hibernation.
2. The box should then be covered with a wire screen, which will protect the turtle from any rodents or predators that might want to take advantage of a motionless and helpless animal.
3. When your turtle hasn't eaten for a while and appears ready to hibernate, it should be moved to its winter quarters, most likely a cellar or garage, where the temperature should range between 40° and 45° F.
4. Instead of feeding the turtle, you should bathe it every day in warm water, to encourage the turtle to empty its intestines in preparation for its long winter sleep.
5. Here the turtle should be placed in a well-ventilated box whose bottom is covered with a moisture-absorbing layer of clay beads, and then filled three-fourths full with almost dry peat moss or wood chips, into which the turtle will burrow and sleep for several months.

The best order is

A. 1 4 3 5 2
B. 3 4 2 5 1
C. 3 2 4 1 5
D. 4 5 2 3 1

Question 18

1. Once he has reached the nest, the hunter uses two sturdy bamboo poles like huge chopsticks to pull the nest away from the mountainside, into a large basket that will be lowered to people waiting below.
2. The world's largest honeybees colonize the Nepalese mountainsides, building honeycombs as large as a person on sheer rock faces that are often hundreds of feet high.
3. In the remote mountain country of Nepal, a small band of "honey hunters" carry out a tradition so ancient that 10,000 year-old drawings of the practice have been found in the caves of Nepal.
4. To harvest the honey and beeswax from these combs, a honey hunter climbs above the nests, lowers a long bamboo-fiber ladder over the cliff, and then climbs down.
5. Throughout this dangerous practice, the hunter is stung repeatedly, and only the veterans, with skin that has been toughened over the years, are able to return from a hunt without the painful swelling caused by stings.

The best order is

A. 2 4 3 5 1
B. 2 4 1 5 3
C. 5 3 2 4 1
D. 3 2 4 1 5

Question 19

1. After the Romans left Britain, there were relentless attacks on the islands from the barbarian tribes of northern Germany—the Angles, Saxons, and Jutes.
2. As the empire weakened, Roman soldiers withdrew from Britain, leaving behind a country that continued to practice the Christian religion that had been introduced by the Romans.
3. Early Latin writings tell of a Christian warrior named Arturius (Arthur, in English) who led the British citizens to defeat these barbarian invaders, and brought an extended period of peace to the lands of Britain.
4. Long ago, the British Isles were part of the far-flung Roman Empire that extended across most of Europe and into Africa and Asia.
5. The romantic legend of King Arthur and his knights of the Round Table, one of the most popular and widespread stories of all time, appears to have some foundation in history.

The best order is

A. 5 4 3 2 1
B. 5 4 2 1 3
C. 4 5 2 3 1
D. 4 3 2 1 5

Question 20

1. The cylinder was allowed to cool until it sould stand on its own, and then it was cut from the tube and split down the side with a single straight cut.
2. Nineteenth-century glassmakers, who had not yet discovered the glazier's modern techniques for making panes of glass, had to create a method for converting their blown glass into flat sheets.
3. The bubble was then pierced at the end to make a hole that opened up while the glassmaker gently spun it, creating a cylinder of glass.
4. Turned on its side and laid on a conveyor belt, the cylinder was strengthened, or tempered, by being heated again and cooled very slowly, eventually flattening out into a single rectangular piece of glass.
5. To do this, the glassmaker dipped the end of a long tube into melted glass and blew into the other end of the tube, creating an expanding bubble of glass.

The best order is

A. 2 5 3 4 1
B. 2 4 5 3 1
C. 3 5 2 4 1
D. 3 1 4 5 2

Question 21   21.____

1. The splints are almost always hidden, but horses are occasionally born whose splinted toes project from the leg on either side, just above the hoof.
2. The second and fourth toes remained, but shrank to thin splints of bone that fused invisibly to the horse's leg bone.
3. Horses are unique among mammals, having evolved feet that each end in what is essentially a single toe, capped by a large, sturdy hoof.
4. Julius Caesar, an emperor of ancient Rome, was said to have owned one of these three-toed horses, and considered it so special that he would not permit anyone else to ride it.
5. Though the horse's earlier ancestors possessed the traditional mammalian set of five toes on each foot, the horse has retained only its third toe; its first and fifth toes disappeared completely as the horse evolved.

The best order is

A. 3 5 2 1 4
B. 5 3 2 4 1
C. 3 2 5 1 4
D. 5 2 3 1 4

Question 22   22.____

1. The new building materials—some of which are twenty feet long, and weigh nearly six tons—were transported to Pohnpei on rafts, and were brought into their present position by using hibiscus fiber ropes and leverage to move the stone columns upward along the inclined trunks of coconut palm trees.
2. The ancestors built great fires to heat the stone, and then poured cool seawater on the columns, which caused the stone to contract and split along natural fracture lines.
3. The now-abandoned enclave of Nan Madol, a group of 92 man-made islands off the shore of the Micronesian island of Pohnpei, is estimated to have been built around the year 500 A.D.
4. The islanders say their ancestors quarried stone columns from a nearby island, where large basalt columns were formed by the cooling of molten lava.
5. The structures of Nan Madol are remarkable for the sheer size of some of the stone "logs" or columns that were used to create the walls of the offshore community, and today anthropologists can only rely on the information of existing local people for clues about how Nan Madol was built.

The best order is

A. 5 4 3 2 1
B. 5 3 1 4 2
C. 3 5 4 2 1
D. 3 1 4 2 5

Question 23

1. One of the most easily manipulated substances on earth, glass can be made into ceramic tiles that are composed of over 90% air.
2. NASA's space shuttles are the first spacecraft ever designed to leave and re-enter the earth's atmosphere while remaining intact.
3. These ceramic tiles are such effective insulators that when a tile emerges from the oven in which it was fired, it can be held safely in a person's hand by the edges while its interior still glows at a temperature well over 2000° F.
4. Eventually, the engineers were led to a material that is as old as our most ancient civilizations—glass.
5. Because the temperature during atmospheric re-entry is so incredibly hot, it took NASA's engineers some time to find a substance capable of protecting the shuttles.

The best order is

A. 5 2 1 3 4
B. 2 5 4 1 3
C. 2 3 1 2 5
D. 5 4 3 1 2

Question 24

1. The secret to teaching any parakeet to talk is patience, and the understanding that when a bird "talks," it is simply imitating what it hears, rather than putting ideas into words.
2. You should stay just out of sight of the bird and repeat the phrase you want it to learn, for at least fifteen minutes every morning and evening.
3. It is important to leave the bird without any words of encouragement or farewell; otherwise it might combine stray remarks or phrases, such as "Good night," with the phrase you are trying to teach it.
4. For this reason, to train your bird to imitate your words you should keep it free of any distractions, especially other noises, while you are giving it "lessons."
5. After your repetition, you should quietly leave the bird alone for a while, to think over what it has just heard.

The best order is

A. 1 4 2 5 3
B. 1 2 4 3 5
C. 3 2 1 5 4
D. 3 1 5 4 2

Question 25

1. As a school approaches, fishermen from neighboring communities join their fishing boats together as a fleet, and string their gill nets together to make a huge fence that is held up by cork floats.
2. At a signal from the party leaders, or *nakura,* the family members pound the sides of the boats or beat the water with long poles, creating a sudden and deafening noise.
3. The fishermen work together to drag the trap into a half-circle that may reach 300 yards in diameter, and then the families move their boats to form the other half of the circle around the school of fish.
4. The school of fish flee from the commotion into the awaiting trap, where a final wall of net is thrown over the open end of the half-circle, securing the day's haul.
5. Indonesian people from the area around the Sulu islands live on the sea, in floating villages made of lashed-together or stilted homes, and make much of their living by fishing their home waters for migrating schools of snapper, scad, and other fish.

The best order is

A. 1 5 3 4 2
B. 1 2 4 3 5
C. 5 1 2 3 4
D. 5 1 3 2 4

KEY (CORRECT ANSWERS)

1. D
2. D
3. B
4. A
5. C

6. C
7. D
8. D
9. A
10. B

11. C
12. A
13. D
14. C
15. D

16. C
17. A
18. D
19. B
20. A

21. A
22. C
23. B
24. A
25. D

PREPARING WRITTEN MATERIALS

EXAMINATION SECTION
TEST 1

DIRECTIONS: Each question or incomplete statement is followed by several suggested answers or completions. Select the one that BEST answers the question or completes the statement. *PRINT THE LETTER OF THE CORRECT ANSWER IN THE SPACE AT THE RIGHT.*

Questions 1-25.

DIRECTIONS: Questions 1 through 25 consist of sentences which may or may not be examples of good English usage. Consider grammar, punctuation, spelling, capitalization, awkwardness, etc. Examine each sentence, and then choose the correct statement about it from the four choices below it. If the English usage in the sentence given is better than it would be with any of the changes suggested in options B, C, and D, choose option A. Do not choose an option that will change the meaning of the sentence.

1. According to Judge Frank, the grocer's sons found guilty of assault and sentenced last Thursday.   1.____

    A. This is an example of acceptable writing.
    B. A comma should be placed after the word *sentenced*.
    C. The word *were* should be placed after *sons*.
    D. The apostrophe in *grocer's* should be placed after the *s*.

2. The department heads assistant said that the stenographers should type duplicate copies of all contracts, leases, and bills.   2.____

    A. This is an example of acceptable writing.
    B. A comma should be placed before the word *contracts*.
    C. An apostrophe should be placed before the *s* in *heads*.
    D. Quotation marks should be placed before *the stenographers* and after *bills*.

3. The lawyers questioned the men to determine who was the true property owner?   3.____

    A. This is an example of acceptable writing.
    B. The phrase *questioned the men* should be changed to *asked the men questions*.
    C. The word *was* should be changed to *were*.
    D. The question mark should be changed to a period.

4. The terms stated in the present contract are more specific than those stated in the previous contract.   4.____

    A. This is an example of acceptable writing.
    B. The word *are* should be changed to *is*.
    C. The word *than* should be changed to *then*.
    D. The word *specific* should be changed to *specified*.

5. Of the few lawyers considered, the one who argued more skillful was chosen for the job.　5.____

   A. This is an example of acceptable writing.
   B. The word *more* should be replaced by the word *most*.
   C. The word *skillful* should be replaced by the word *skillfully*.
   D. The word *chosen* should be replaced by the word *selected*.

6. Each of the states has a court of appeals; some states have circuit courts.　6.____

   A. This is an example of acceptable writing.
   B. The semi-colon should be changed to a comma.
   C. The word *has* should be changed to *have*.
   D. The word *some* should be capitalized.

7. The court trial has greatly effected the child's mental condition.　7.____

   A. This is an example of acceptable writing.
   B. The word *effected* should be changed to *affected*.
   C. The word *greatly* should be placed after *effected*.
   D. The apostrophe in *child's* should be placed after the *s*.

8. Last week, the petition signed by all the officers was sent to the Better Business Bureau.　8.____

   A. This is an example of acceptable writing.
   B. The phrase *last week* should be placed after *officers*.
   C. A comma should be placed after *petition*.
   D. The word *was* should be changed to *were*.

9. Mr. Farrell claims that he requested form A-12, and three booklets describing court procedures.　9.____

   A. This is an example of acceptable writing.
   B. The word *that* should be eliminated.
   C. A colon should be placed after *requested*.
   D. The comma after *A-12* should be eliminated.

10. We attended a staff conference on Wednesday the new safety and fire rules were discussed.　10.____

    A. This is an example of acceptable writing.
    B. The words *safety, fire,* and *rules* should begin with capital letters.
    C. There should be a comma after the word *Wednesday*.
    D. There should be a period after the word *Wednesday,* and the word *the* should begin with a capital letter.

11. Neither the dictionary or the telephone directory could be found in the office library.　11.____

    A. This is an example of acceptable writing.
    B. The word *or* should be changed to *nor*.
    C. The word *library* should be spelled *libery*.
    D. The word *neither* should be changed to *either*.

12. The report would have been typed correctly if the typist could read the draft.   12._____

    A. This is an example of acceptable writing.
    B. The word *would* should be removed.
    C. The word *have* should be inserted after the word *could*.
    D. The word *correctly* should be changed to *correct*.

13. The supervisor brought the reports and forms to an employees desk.   13._____

    A. This is an example of acceptable writing.
    B. The word *brought* should be changed to *took*.
    C. There should be a comma after the word *reports* and a comma after the word *forms*.
    D. The word *employees* should be spelled *employee's*.

14. It's important for all the office personnel to submit their vacation schedules on time.   14._____

    A. This is an example of acceptable writing.
    B. The word *It's* should be spelled *Its*.
    C. The word *their* should be spelled *they're*.
    D. The word *personnel* should be spelled *personal*.

15. The supervisor wants that all staff members report to the office at 9:00 A.M.   15._____

    A. This is an example of acceptable writing.
    B. The word *that* should be removed and the word *to* should be inserted after the word *members*.
    C. There should be a comma after the word *wants* and a comma after the word *office*.
    D. The word *wants* should be changed to *want*, and the word *shall* should be inserted after the word *members*.

16. Every morning the clerk opens the office mail and distributes it.   16._____

    A. This is an example of acceptable writing.
    B. The word *opens* should be changed to *open*.
    C. The word *mail* should be changed to *letters*.
    D. The word *it* should be changed to *them*.

17. The secretary typed more fast on a desktop computer than on a tablet.   17._____

    A. This is an example of acceptable writing.
    B. The words *more fast* should be changed to *faster*.
    C. There should be a comma after the words *desktop computer*.
    D. The word *than* should be changed to *then*.

18. The typist used an extention cord in order to connect her typewriter to the outlet nearest to her desk.   18._____

    A. This is an example of acceptable writing.
    B. A period should be placed after the word *cord*, and the word *in* should have a capital *I*.
    C. A comma should be placed after the word *typewriter*.
    D. The word *extention* should be spelled *extension*.

19. He would have went to the conference if he had received an invitation.

    A. This is an example of acceptable writing.
    B. The word *went* should be replaced by the word *gone*.
    C. The word *had* should be replaced by *would have*.
    D. The word *conference* should be spelled *conferance*.

20. In order to make the report neater, he spent many hours rewriting it.

    A. This is an example of acceptable writing.
    B. The word *more* should be inserted before the word *neater*.
    C. There should be a colon after the word *neater*.
    D. The word *spent* should be changed to *have spent*.

21. His supervisor told him that he should of read the memorandum more carefully.

    A. This is an example of acceptable writing.
    B. The word *memorandum* should be spelled *memorandom*.
    C. The word *of* should be replaced by the word *have*.
    D. The word *carefully* should be replaced by the word *careful*.

22. It was decided that two separate reports should be written.

    A. This is an example of acceptable writing.
    B. A comma should be inserted after the word *decided*.
    C. The word *be* should be replaced by the word *been*.
    D. A colon should be inserted after the word *that*.

23. She don't seem to understand that the work must be done as soon as possible.

    A. This is an example of acceptable writing.
    B. The word *doesn't* should replace the word *don't*.
    C. The word *why* should replace the word *that*.
    D. The word *as* before the word *soon* should be eliminated.

24. He excepted praise from his supervisor for a job well done.

    A. This is an example of acceptable writing.
    B. The word *excepted* should be spelled *accepted*.
    C. The order of the words *well done* should be changed to *done well*.
    D. There should be a comma after the word *supervisor*.

25. What appears to be intentional errors in grammar occur several times in the passage.

    A. This is an example of acceptable writing.
    B. The word *occur* should be spelled *occurr*.
    C. The word *appears* should be changed to *appear*.
    D. The phrase *several times* should be changed to *from time to time*.

KEY (CORRECT ANSWERS)

1. C
2. C
3. D
4. A
5. C

6. A
7. B
8. A
9. D
10. D

11. B
12. C
13. D
14. A
15. B

16. A
17. B
18. D
19. B
20. A

21. C
22. A
23. B
24. B
25. C

TEST 2

DIRECTIONS: Each question consists of a sentence which may or may not be an example of good formal English usage. Examine each sentence, considering grammar, punctuation, spelling, capitalization, and awkwardness. Then choose the CORRECT statement about it from the four options below it. If the English usage in the sentence given is better than any of the changes suggested in options B, C, or D, pick option A. Do not pick an option that will change the meaning of the sentence. *PRINT THE LETTER OF THE CORRECT ANSWER IN THE SPACE AT THE RIGHT.*

1. I don't know who could possibly of broken it.

   A. This is an example of acceptable writing.
   B. The word *who* should be replaced by the word *whom*.
   C. The word *of* should be replaced by the word *have*.
   D. The word *broken* should be replaced by the word *broke*.

2. Telephoning is easier than to write.

   A. This is an example of acceptable writing.
   B. The word *telephoning* should be spelled *telephoneing*.
   C. The word *than* should be replaced by the word *then*.
   D. The words *to write* should be replaced by the word *writing*.

3. The two operators who have been assigned to these consoles are on vacation.

   A. This is an example of acceptable writing.
   B. A comma should be placed after the word *operators*.
   C. The word *who* should be replaced by the word *whom*.
   D. The word *are* should be replaced by the word *is*.

4. You were suppose to teach me how to operate a plugboard.

   A. This is an example of acceptable writing.
   B. The word *were* should be replaced by the word *was*.
   C. The word *suppose* should be replaced by the word *supposed*.
   D. The word *teach* should be replaced by the word *learn*.

5. If you had taken my advice; you would have spoken with him.

   A. This is an example of acceptable writing.
   B. The word *advice* should be spelled *advise*.
   C. The words *had taken* should be replaced by the word *take*.
   D. The semicolon should be changed to a comma.

6. The clerk could have completed the assignment on time if he knows where these materials were located.

   A. This is an example of acceptable writing.
   B. The word *knows* should be replaced by *had known*.
   C. The word *were* should be replaced by *had been*.
   D. The words *where these materials were located* should be replaced by *the location of these materials*.

2 (#2)

7. All employees should be given safety training. Not just those who have accidents. 7._____

   A. This is an example of acceptable writing.
   B. The period after the word *training* should be changed to a colon.
   C. The period after the word *training* should be changed to a semicolon, and the first letter of the word *Not* should be changed to a small *n*.
   D. The period after the word *training* should be changed to a comma, and the first letter of the word *Not* should be changed to a small *n*.

8. This proposal is designed to promote employee awareness of the suggestion program, to encourage employee participation in the program, and to increase the number of suggestions submitted. 8._____

   A. This is an example of acceptable writing.
   B. The word *proposal* should be spelled *preposal*.
   C. The words *to increase the number of suggestions submitted* should be changed to *an increase in the number of suggestions is expected*.
   D. The word *promote* should be changed to *enhance,* and the word *increase* should be changed to *add to*.

9. The introduction of inovative managerial techniques should be preceded by careful analysis of the specific circumstances and conditions in each department. 9._____

   A. This is an example of acceptable writing.
   B. The word *techniques* should be spelled *techneques*.
   C. The word *inovative* should be spelled *innovative*.
   D. A comma should be placed after the word *circumstances* and after the word *conditions*.

10. This occurrence indicates that such criticism embarrasses him. 10._____

    A. This is an example of acceptable writing.
    B. The word *occurrence* should be spelled *occurence*.
    C. The word *criticism* should be spelled *criticism*.
    D. The word *embarrasses* should be spelled *embarasses*.

11. He can recommend a mechanic whose work is reliable. 11._____

    A. This is an example of acceptable writing.
    B. The word *reliable* should be spelled *relyable*.
    C. The word *whose* should be spelled *who's*.
    D. The word *mechanic* should be spelled *mecanic*.

12. She typed quickly; like someone who had not a moment to lose. 12._____

    A. This is an example of acceptable writing.
    B. The word *not* should be removed.
    C. The semicolon should be changed to a comma.
    D. The word *quickly* should be placed before instead of after the word *typed*.

13. She insisted that she had to much work to do. 13._____

    A. This is an example of acceptable writing.
    B. The word *insisted* should be spelled *insisted*.

C. The word *to* used in front of *much* should be spelled *too*.
D. The word *do* should be changed to *be done*.

14. The report, along with the accompanying documents, were submitted for review. 14.____

    A. This is an example of acceptable writing.
    B. The words *were submitted* should be changed to *was submitted*.
    C. The word *accompanying* should be spelled *accompaning*.
    D. The comma after the word *report* should be taken out.

15. If others must use your files, be certain that they understand how the system works, but insist that you do all the filing and refiling. 15.____

    A. This is an example of acceptable writing.
    B. There should be a period after the word *works*, and the word *but* should start a new sentence.
    C. The words *filing* and *refiling* should be spelled *fileing* and *refileing*.
    D. There should be a comma after the word *but*.

16. The appeal was not considered because of its late arrival. 16.____

    A. This is an example of acceptable writing.
    B. The word *its* should be changed to *it's*.
    C. The word *its* should be changed to *the*.
    D. The words *late arrival* should be changed to *arrival late*.

17. The letter must be read carefuly to determine under which subject it should be filed. 17.____

    A. This is an example of acceptable writing.
    B. The word *under* should be changed to *at*.
    C. The word *determine* should be spelled *determin*.
    D. The word *carefuly* should be spelled *carefully*.

18. He showed potential as an office manager, but he lacked skill in delegating work. 18.____

    A. This is an example of acceptable writing.
    B. The word *delegating* should be spelled *delagating*.
    C. The word *potential* should be spelled *potencial*.
    D. The words *he lacked* should be changed to *was lacking*.

19. His supervisor told him that it would be all right to receive personal mail at the office. 19.____

    A. This is an example of acceptable writing.
    B. The words *all right* should be changed to *alright*.
    C. The word *personal* should be spelled *personel*.
    D. The word *mail* should be changed to *letters*.

20. The report, along with the accompanying documents, were submitted for review. 20.____

    A. This is an example of acceptable writing.
    B. The words *were submitted* should be changed to *was submitted*.
    C. The word *accompanying* should be spelled *accompaning*.
    D. The comma after the word *report* should be taken out.

KEY (CORRECT ANSWERS)

1.	C	11.	A
2.	D	12.	C
3.	A	13.	C
4.	C	14.	B
5.	D	15.	A
6.	B	16.	A
7.	D	17.	D
8.	A	18.	A
9.	C	19.	A
10.	A	20.	B

THE ENGLISH AND METRIC SYSTEMS OF MEASUREMENT

TABLE OF CONTENTS

	Page
A. THE ENGLISH SYSTEM	1
1. Linear (Line or Long) Measure	1
2. Square (Surface) Measure	1
3. Cubic Measure	1
4. Circular or Angular Measure	2
5. Liquid Measure	2
6. Dry Measure	2
7. Avoirdupois Weight	2
8. Troy Weight	3
9. Apothecaries' Dry Weight and Liquid Measure	3
10. Time Table	3
11. Counting Table	4
12. Paper Measure	4
13. Measure of Value	4
14. Commodity Weights	4
15. Bushel Weights	4
B. THE METRIC SYSTEM	5
I. METRIC TABLES	5
1. Linear Measure	5
2. Square Measure	5
3. Cubic Measure	5
4. Liquid and Dry Measure	5
5. Weight Table	5
II. METRIC AND ENGLISH EQUIVALENTS	6
1. Linear Measure Equivalents	6
2. Square Measure Equivalents	6
3. Cubic Measure Equivalents	6
4. Liquid and Dry Measure Equivalents	6
5. Weight Measure Equivalents	6
III. THE RELATIONSHIP OF AMERICAN AND METRIC UNITS	6

THE ENGLISH AND METRIC SYSTEMS OF MEASUREMENT

A. The English System. Tables of weights and measures have been established by law and custom. These units of measurement are concrete numbers commonly referred to as *denominate numbers*.

1. LINEAR (LINE OR LONG) MEASURE

Used in measuring distances and lengths, widths, or thicknesses.

12 inches (in.)	= 1 foot (ft.)
3 feet	= 1 yard (yd.)
5 1/2 yards, or 16 1/2 feet	= 1 rod (rd.)
40 rods	= 1 furlong (fur.).
8 furlongs, or 320 rods	= 1 mile (mi.)

The unit of length is the yard.
1 hand = 4 inches (used in measuring the height of horses).
1 fathom (marine measure) = 6 feet (used in measuring depths at sea).
1 knot = 1.152 1/2 miles (nautical or geographical mile).
1 league = 3 knots (3 X 1.15 miles).

2. SQUARE (SURFACE) MEASURE

Used in measuring areas of surfaces.

144 square inches (sq. in.)	= 1 square foot (sq. ft.)
9 square feet	= 1 square yard (sq. yd.)
30 1/4 square yards	= 1 square rod (sq. rd.)
160 square rods	= 1 acre (A.)
640 acres	= 1 square mile (sq. mi.)

The unit in measuring land is the acre, except for city lots.
A square, used in roofing, is 100 square feet.
The unit in measuring other surfaces is the square yard.

3. CUBIC MEASURE

Used in measuring the volume of a body or a solid as well as the contents or capacity of hollow bodies.

1,728 cubic inches (cu. in.)	= 1 cubic foot (cu. ft.)
27 cubic feet	= 1 cubic yard (cu. yd.)
231 cubic inches	= 1 gallon (gal.)
24 3/4 cubic feet	= 1 perch (P.)
128 cubic feet	= 1 cord (cd.)
1 cubic foot	= 7 1/2 gallons

1 cubic yard of earth = 1 load.
A cord of wood (128 cubic feet) is a pile 8 feet long, 4 feet wide, and 4 feet high.
1 cubic foot of water weighs 62 1/2 pounds (avoirdupois).

4. CIRCULAR OR ANGULAR MEASURE

Used in measuring angles or areas of circles.

60 seconds (")	= 1 minute (')	30 degrees = 1 sign (1/12 of a circle)
60 minutes	= 1 degree (°)	60 degrees = 1 sextant (1/6 of a circle)
360 degrees	= 1 circle (cir.)	90 degrees = 1 quadrant (1/4 of a circle)

A 90° angle is a right angle.

5. LIQUID MEASURE

Used in measuring the liquid capacity of vessels or containers of all liquids except medicine.

4 gills (gi.)	= 1 pint (pt.)	63 gallons	= 1 hogshead (hhd.)
2 pints	= 1 quart (qt.)	2 barrels	= 1 hogshead
4 quarts	= 1 gallon (gal.)	7 1/2 gallons	= 1 cubic foot
31 1/2 gallons	= 1 barrel (bbl.)		

The unit of liquid measure is the United States gallon of 231 cubic inches.
1 gallon of water weighs 8 1/3 pounds (avoirdupois).

6. DRY MEASURE

Used in measuring the volume of the contents of containers of solids, such as produce, seed, fruits, etc., that are not sold by weight.

2 pints (pt.)	= 1 quart (qt.)	4 pecks	= 1 bushel (bu.)
8 quarts	= 1 peck (pk.)	2 3/4 bushels	= 1 barrel

7. AVOIRDUPOIS WEIGHT

Used in weighing heavy, coarse articles, such as coal, iron, grain, hay, etc.

16 ounces (oz.)	= 1 pound (lb.)
100 pounds	= 1 hundredweight (cwt.)
20 hundredweights	= 1 ton (T.)
2,000 pounds	= 1 ton
2,240 pounds	= 1 long or gross ton
7,000 grains (gr.)	= 1 pound avoirdupois

The United States Government uses the long ton of 2,240 pounds in fixing the duty on merchandise that is taxed by the ton.

Coal and iron sold at the mine are also weighed by the long ton.

8. TROY WEIGHT

Used in weighing precious minerals, and by the United States Government in weighing coins.

24 grains	= 1 pennyweight (pwt.)
20 pennyweights	= 1 ounce
12 ounces	= 1 pound
240 pennyweights	= 1 pound
5,760 grains	= 1 pound troy
3,168 grains	= 1 carat

The unit of weight in the United States is the troy pound.

Pure gold is 24 carats fine. Gold marked 14 carats is 14/24, by weight, pure gold and 10/24, by weight, alloy.

9. APOTHECARIES' DRY WEIGHT AND LIQUID MEASURE

Used by druggists and physicians in weighing and measuring drugs and chemicals, and in compounding dry and liquid medicines.

APOTHECARIES' DRY WEIGHT

20 grains	= 1 scruple (sc.)
3 scruples	= 1 dram (dr.)
8 drams	= 1 ounce (oz.)
12 ounces	= 1 pound (lb.)

APOTHECARIES' FLUID MEASURE

60 minims (m.)	= 1 fluid drachm, or dram (f3)
8 fluid drachms	= 1 fluid ounce (f3)
16 fluid ounces	= 1 pint (O.)
8 pints	= 1 gallon (Cong.)

Avoirdupois weight is used when drugs and chemicals are bought and sold wholesale.

10. TIME TABLE

60 seconds (sec.)	= 1 minute (min.)	52 weeks	= 1 year (yr.)
60 minutes	= 1 hour (hr.)	12 months	= 1 year
24 hours	= 1 day (da.)	365 days	= 1 year*
7 days	=1 week (wk.)	100 years	= 1 century (C.)
30 days	=1 month (mo.)*		

* January, 31 days; February, 28 days (29 days in February in a leap year of 366 days); March, 31 days; April, 30 days; May, 31 days; June, 30 days; July, 31 days; August, 31 days; September, 30 days; October, 31 days; November, 30 days; December, 31 days.

11. COUNTING TABLE

20 units	= 1 score
12 units	= 1 dozen
12 dozen	= 1 gross (gro.)
12 gross	= 1 great gross (gr. gro.)

12. PAPER MEASURE

24 sheets	= 1 quire (qr.)
20 quires	= 1 ream (rm.)
2 reams	= 1 bundle (bdl.)
5 bundles	= 1 bale (bl.)

13. MEASURES OF VALUE

United States Money

10 mills	= 1 cent
10 cents	= 1 dime
10 dimes	= 1 dollar
10 dollars	= 1 eagle

The unit of measure is the dollar.

English Money

4 farthings (far.)	= 1 penny (d)
12 pence	= 1 shilling (s.)
20 shillings	= 1 pound sterling ()

The unit of measure is the pound sterling.

French Money

10 millimes (m.)	= 1 centime (c.)
10 centimes	= 1 decime (dc.)
10 decimes	= 1 franc (F.)

The unit of measure is the franc.

German Money

100 pfennig (pf.)	= 1 mark

The unit of measure is the mark.

14. COMMODITY WEIGHTS

Beef, barrel	200	lbs.	Nails, keg	100	lbs.
Butter, firkin	56	lbs.	Pork, barrel	200	lbs.
Flour, barrel	196	lbs.	Salt, barrel	280	lbs.

15. BUSHEL WEIGHTS

The following weights are used in a bushel in most of the states:

Barley	48 lbs.	Corn (shelled)	56 lbs.	Potatoes	60 lbs.
Beans	60 lbs.	Corn meal	48 lbs.	Rye	56 lbs.
Buckwheat	48 lbs.	Oats	32 lbs.	Sweet potatoes	54 lbs.
Clover seed	60 lbs.	Onions	57 lbs.	Timothy seed	45 lbs.
Corn (ear)	70 lbs.	Peas	60 lbs.	Wheat	60 lbs.

B. The Metric System. The metric system of weights and measures is a decimal system. The three principal units are

1. The meter, which is the unit of length.
2. The liter, which is the unit of capacity.
3. The gram, which is the unit of weight or mass.

The basic unit of the metric system is the meter, upon which the other units are based. The length of the meter, which is 39.37 inches, was originally determined by taking one ten-millionth of the distance from the equator to the pole.

I. METRIC TABLES
1. LINEAR MEASURE

10 millimeters (mm.)	= 1 centimeter (cm.)
10 centimeters	= 1 decimeter (dm.)
10 decimeters	= 1 meter (m.)
10 meters	= 1 decameter (Dm.)
10 decameters	= 1 hectometer (Hm.)
10 hectometers	= 1 kilometer (Km.)
10 kilometers	= 1 myriameter (Mm.)

The unit of measures of length is the meter.

2. SQUARE MEASURE

100 square millimeters (sq. mm.)	= 1 square centimeter (sq. cm.)
100 square centimeters	= 1 square decimeter (sq. dm.)
100 square decimeters	= 1 square meter (sq. m.)
100 square meters	= 1 square decameter (sq. Dm.)
100 square decameters	= 1 square hectometer (sq. Hm.)
100 square hectometers	= 1 square kilometer (sq. Km.)

The unit of square measures is the square meter.

3. CUBIC MEASURE

1,000 cubic millimeters (cu. mm.)	= 1 cubic centimeter (cu. cm.)
1,000 cubic centimeters	= 1 cubic decimeter (cu. dm.)
1,000 cubic decimeters	= 1 cubic meter (cu. m.)
1,000 cubic meters	= 1 cubic decameter (cu. Dm.)
1,000 cubic decameters	= 1 cubic hectometer (cu. Hm.)
1,000 cubic hectometers	= 1 cubic kilometer (cu. Km.)

The unit of measures of volume is the cubic meter.

4. LIQUID AND DRY MEASURE

10 milliliters (ml.)	= 1 centiliter (cl.)	10 liters	= 1 decaliter (Dl.)
10 centiliters	= 1 deciliter (dl.)	10 decaliters	= 1 hectoliter (Hl.)
10 deciliters	= 1 liter (1.)	10 hectoliters	= 1 kiloliter (Kl.)

The unit of capacity for liquids and solids is the liter.

5. WEIGHT TABLE

10 milligrams (mg.)	= 1 centigram (eg.)
10 centigrams	= 1 decigram (dg.)
10 decigrams	= 1 gram (g.)
10 grams	= 1 decagram (Dg.)
10 decagrams	= 1 hectogram (Hg.)
10 hectograms	= 1 kilogram (Kg.)
10 kilograms	= 1 myriagram (Mg.)
10 myriagrams	= 1 quintal (Q.)
10 quintals	= 1 tonneau (T.)

The unit of weight is the gram.

II. METRIC AND ENGLISH EQUIVALENTS
1 LINEAR-MEASURE EQUIVALENTS

1 in.	= 2.54 cm.	1 cm.	=	.3937 in.
1 ft.	= .3048 m.	1 dm.	=	.328 ft.
1 yd.	= .9144 m.	1m.	=	1.0936 yds.
1 rd.	= 5.029 m.	1 Dm.	=	1.9884 rds.
1 mi.	= 1,6093 Km.	1Km.	=	.6214 mi.

2. SQUARE-MEASURE EQUIVALENTS

1 sq. in.	6.452 sq. cm.	1 sq. cm.		155 sq. in.
1 sq. ft.	= .0929 sq. m.	1 sq. dm.		1076 sq.ft.
1 sq. yd.	= .8361 sq. m.	1 sq. m.	=	1 196 sq. yds.
1 sq. rd.	= 25.293 sq. m.	1 a.		3.954 sq. rds.
1 A.	= 40.47 a. (ares)	1 ha.	=	2.471 A.
1 sq. mi.	= 259 ha. (hectares	1 sq. Km.	=	.3861 sq. mi.

3. CUBIC-MEASURE EQUIVALENTS

1 cu. in.	= 16.387 cu. cm.	1 cu. cm.	=	.061 cu. in.
1 cu. ft.	= 28.317 cu. dm.	1 cu. dm.		.0353 cu ft.
1 cu. yd.	= .7646 cu. m.	1 cu. m.	=	1.308 cu. yds.
1 cd.	= 3.624 st. (steres)	1 st.	=	.2759 cd.

4. LIQUID- AND DRY-MEASURE EQUIVALENTS

1 dry qt.	=	1 1011.	1l.	= .908 dry qt.
1 liquid qt.	=	.94631	1l.	= 1.0567 liquid qt.
1 liquid gal.	=	.3785 Dl.	1Dl.	= 2.6417 liquid gal.
1 pk.		.881 Dl.	1Dl.	= 1.135 pk.
1 bu.		..3524 Hl.	1Hl.	= 2.8377 bu.

5. WEIGHT-MEASURE EQUIVALENTS

1 qt. Troy	=	.0648 g.	1 g.	=	15.432 gr. Troy
1 oz. Troy	=	31. 104 g.	1 g.	=	.03215 oz. Troy
1 oz. Avoir.	=	28.35 g.	1 g.	=	.03527 oz. Avoir.
1 lb. Troy		.3732 kg.	1 kg.	=	2.679 lbs. Troy
1 lb. Avoir.	=	.4536 kg.	1 kg.	=	2.2046 lbs. Avoir.
1 T. (short)	=	.9072 1.	1 t.	=	1 1023 T. (short)

III. *THE RELATIONSHIP OF AMERICAN AND METRIC UNITS*

Pounds (avoirdupois)	X	.454	=	Kilograms
Pounds (avoirdupois)	X	453.592	=	Grams
Grams	X	.035	=	Ounces
Ounces	X	28.35	=	Grams
Kilograms	X	2.205	=	Pounds
Grams	X	.002205	=	Pounds
Quarts (liquid)	X	.946	=	Liters
Quarts (liquid)	X	946.333	=	Milliliters
Liters	X	1.057	=	Quarts
Liters	X	1000.	=	Milliliters
Milliliters	X	.001057	=	Quarts

MEASUREMENT RELATIONSHIPS AND PRINCIPLES

1. ENGLISH MEASUREMENT

    <u>Common English Measures</u>

    Length
    - 1 foot (ft) = 12 inches (in)
    - 1 yard (yd) = 3 feet (ft)
    - 1 mile (mi) = 5,280 feet (ft)

    Volume
    - 1 quart (qt) = 2 pints (pt)
    - 1 gallon (gal) = 4 quarts (qts)

    Weight
    - 1 pound (lb) = 16 ounces (oz)
    - 1 ton = 2,000 pounds (lb)

    Time
    - 1 minute (min) = 60 seconds (sec)
    - 1 hour (hr) = 60 minutes (min)
    - 1 day (da) = 24 hours (hr)
    - 1 week (wk) = 7 days (da)
    - 1 year (yr) = 52 weeks (wk) = 365 days (da)

The equivalent measures in the table above should be memorized. Once committed to memory, only an additional knowledge of basic arithmetic is necessary for solving most commonly encountered test problems.

<u>Problem:</u> Change 38 yards to feet

<u>Solution:</u> 1 yard = 3 feet
38 · 1 yard = 38.3 feet
38 yards = 114 feet

<u>Problem:</u> How many pints are in 8 1/2 gallons:

<u>Solution:</u> 1 gallon = 4 quarts
8 1/2 x 1 gallon = 8 1/2 x 4 quarts
8 1/2 gallons = 34 quarts
1 quart = 2 pints
34 x 1 quart = 34 x 2 pints
34 quarts = 68 pints
Thus, 8 1/2 gallons = 34 quarts = 68 pints,
so 8 1/2 gallons = 68 pints.

<u>Problem:</u> A man drives 10 miles in 20 minutes. What was his speed in miles per hour?

<u>Solution:</u> $\dfrac{10 \text{ miles}}{20 \text{ minutes}} \times \dfrac{\overset{3}{60} \text{ minutes}}{1 \text{ hour}}$

$= \dfrac{30 \text{ miles}}{1 \text{ hour}} = 30 \text{ miles per hour}$

Notice how *miles per minute* was converted to *miles per hour*. We multiplied by the unit ratio *60 min/1 hr* (which is like multiplying by an equivalent of $^v(l)$ to cancel the minutes and replace them with *hour*. This is a common technique when miles per hour, cost per pound, and similar ratios are involved.

Problem: The speed of sound is approximately 1,100 feet per second. How many miles per hour is this?

Solution: $$\frac{1100 \text{ feet}}{1 \text{ second}} \times \frac{3600 \text{ second}}{1 \text{ hour}} \times \frac{1 \text{ mile}}{5280 \text{ feet}}$$

$$= \frac{1100 \times 3600}{5280} \frac{\text{mile}}{\text{hour}}$$

750 miles per hour

Here we multiplied by two unit ratios, $\frac{3600 \text{ seconds}}{1 \text{ hour}}$ and $\frac{1 \text{ mile}}{5280 \text{ feet}}$ expressly designed to replace *seconds* by *hours* and *feet* by *miles*. Notice that each of these ratios alone is the equivalent of 1.

Problem: Ten feet of pipe sell for $13.77. At this rate, how much would ten yards cost?

Solution: Since 1 yard = 3 feet, 10 yards = 30 feet. A 10-foot unit sells for $13.77. For 30 feet we need 3 10-foot units: 3 x 13.77 = $41.41

Problem: Assume coffee costs about $4 per pound. Is this more or less than the cost per pound of a new car which sells for $10,000 and weighs 2.3 tons?

Solution: $$\frac{\overset{5}{10,000} \text{ dollars}}{2.3 \text{ tons}} \times \frac{1 \text{ ton}}{2000 \text{ lbs}}$$

$$= \frac{5 \text{ dollars}}{2.3 \text{ lbs}}$$

= $2.18/pound

Here again, in order to solve the problem we multiplied by the equivalent of 1.

The new car costs less per pound than the coffee.

Problem: A recycling center pays 12¢ for every 50 pounds of old newspapers. How much do they pay per ton? 40

Solution: $$\frac{12¢}{50 \text{ lbs}} \times \frac{2000 \text{ lbs}}{1 \text{ ton}}$$

$$= \frac{480¢}{\text{ton}} = \$4.80 \text{ per ton}$$

EXERCISES

1. A glacier moves at a rate of 18 inches per year. How many feet will it move in 25 years?

2. Assume that a gallon of water weighs 8 pounds. What is the weight in tons of the water in a swimming pool that holds 60,000 gallons?

3. Kathy drives 8 miles in 12 minutes. What is her speed in miles per hour?

4. Julio needs 56 yards of white pine boards. These boards sell for 40c per foot. How much will 56 yards cost?

5. A can of cat food holds 6 ounces. How many cans would you need to buy in order to purchase 10 pounds of cat food?

6. A person is 81 inches tall. How many feet tall is this?

7. Four feet of fabric cost $15. At the same rate, how much would you pay for 13 yards of the fabric?

8. You have 10 ropes, each 10 feet in length. How many 9-inch lengths can you get from these 10 ropes?

9. An experiment requires 1/2 pint per student of a certain chemical during a chemistry laboratory. The chemical is sold by the gallon only. How many gallons should be on hand for a class of 43 students?

2. METRIC MEASUREMENT

Common Metric Measures

Length
1 meter (m) = 1000 millimeters (mm)
1 meter (m) = 100 centimeters (cm)
1 kilometer (km) = 1000 meters (m)

Volume
1 liter (l) = 1000 milliliters (ml)

Weight
1 gram (g) = 1000 milligrams (mg)
1 kilogram (kg) = 1000 grams (g)

The information in this table should be memorized. It is helpful to know that the metric system has a well-designed system of prefixes:

kilo means 1000
centi means 1/100
milli means 1/1000

Thus, *kilometer* means *1000 meters*. *Centimeter* means *1/100 of a meter,* so it follows that 100 centimeters make up 1 meter. *Milli* means 1/1000. Thus, a millimeter is 1/1000 of a meter; a milliliter is 1/1000 of a liter; a millogram is 1/1000 of a gram. This is the same as saying that 1000 millimeters equal
1 meter; 1000 milliliters equal 1 liter; 1000 milligrams equal 1 gram.

If there were a metric unit called a *boron,* then a kiloboron would equal 1000 borons, a centiboron would be 1/100 of a boron, and a milliboron would be 1/1000 of a boron. How many milli-borons would it take to make one boron?

The rest of this section is devoted to conversions and problem solving within the metric system.

Problem: Change 250 centimeters to meters.

Solution: 1 centimeter = 1/100 meter = .01 meter
So, 250 cm = 250 .01 m
250 cm = 2.50 m

The preceding example illustrates an important point: Nearly all metric conversions can be accomplished by moving a decimal point. Since centimeters and meters are related by 1/100 or 100, the decimal point moves two places - to the left for centimeters to meters (moving from a smaller unit to a larger one) and to the right for meters to centimeters (moving from a larger unit to a smaller unit).

centimeters - → meters: 476 cm = 4.75 m
meters - → centimeters: 3.6 m = 360 cm

Note that the decimal point moves to the left when converting from smaller to larger units. It moves right when converting from larger to smaller units.

How many places would you move the decimal point for meter/ millimeter conversions? Since 1 meter = 1000 millimeters (or 1 millimeter = 1/1000 meter), the decimal point moves 3 places.

millimeters - → meters: 3700 mm = 3.7 m
meters - → milliliters: .5 m = 500 mm

Likewise,

milliliters - → liters: 260 ml = .26 l
liters - → milliliters: 3.71 l = 3710 ml
milligrams - → grams: 34.6 mg = .0346 g
grams - → milligrams: 34 g = 34000 mg

How about meter/kilometer conversions or gram/kilogram conversions? Since a kilometer equals 1000 meters and a kilogram equals 1000 grams, the conversions also involve multiplying or dividing by 1000, that is, by moving the decimal point 3 places.

meter - → kilometer: 3500 m = 3.500 km
kilometer - → meter: .25 km = 250 m
gram - → kilogram: 200 g = .2 kg

kilogram ⟶ gram: 1.5 kg = 1500 g

Problem: Change 2.6 centimeters to millimeters.
Solution: According to the metric table,
           100 cm = 1 m = 1000 mm
           Thus, 1 cm = 10 mm
           But if 1 cm = 10 mm,
           then, 2.6 cm = 26 mm.

(Notice, again, that you only need to move the decimal point. You move it one place this time since centimeters and millimeters are related by a factor of 10 or by a factor of 1/10, depending on the direction of the change.)

EXERCISES

10. A bottle holds 0.3 liters. How many milliliters is this?

11. A can of pineapples weighs 400 grams. How many kilograms is this? How many milligrams?

12. Paul is 1.7 m tall. What is his height in cm?

13. A glacier moves at the rate of 31 cm per year. How many meters will it move in a century?

14. At a cost of 32¢ for 5 grams, how much would you pay for half a kilogram?

15. How many 15 cm lengths can be cut from a strand of material 3 m long?

16. How many 750 ml wine bottles will it take to exceed the contents of 7 bottles each holding 1 liter?

17. When nerves are severed and then reattached on the operating table, they regenerate themselves at the rate of 1 mm/day. Dan cut his forearm at a point 21.5 cm from his fingertips. How many days after surgery will it be before sensation returns to his fingertips?

18. At a rate of $42/m, what would be the total cost of paving a stretch of road which is 3.6 km long?

19. Paul is charged $3.20 for 250 ml of a particular medicine. If he takes two ml doses per day, what
    a. is his approximate cost per day?
    b. is the cost of 4 liters of this medicine?

3. ENGLISH AND METRIC MEASUREMENTS

Most people are familiar with the relative sizes and uses of the common English measures discussed in Section 1 above. This section includes some exercises involving English measures but the discussion that follows will focus on the less familiar metric units.

A meter is slightly longer than a yard. A person who is two meters tall is looked up to by most people. A centimeter is 1/100 of a meter and forms the major subdivisions on a meter-stick. The width of the fingernail on your little finger is probably about 1 cm. A pencil is slightly less than 1 cm in diameter. A millimeter is 1/10 the size of a centimeter and is roughly equal to the thickness of a dime. A kilometer (1000 meters) is slightly more than 1/2 mile (1 km roughly equals 5/8 miles).

A liter is roughly the same as a quart. A milliliter, is one thousand times smaller. Wine is often sold in 750 ml bottles (which are the same as 0.75 1 bottles). A teaspoon holds about 5 ml.

The basic metric unit of weight, 1 gram, is roughly the weight of a paperclip. As a rule, only light objects have their weights expressed in grams. A candy bar might weigh 30 grams. Far more common are kilogram weights. A kilogram is more than 2 pounds. A 220-pound football player weighs 100 kilograms. However, human weights of 50, 60, 70, and 80 kg are more common. Conversely, milligram weights are very small; they are most often encountered in scientific fields.

The metric unit of temperature is the degree Celsius. Water freezes at $^\circ$ C and boils at 100° C. A comfortable outdoor temperature is somewhere in the upper 20° C. Normal body temperature is about 37° C.

EXERCISES

20. For each of the following items, identify the approximate measurement from the choices given.

    a. Family car (feet): 3, 7, 14, 28
    b. Arm length (feet): 1, 3, 6, 12
    c. Big toe width (inches): 1/2, 1, 1 1/2, 2
    d. Record album width (inches): 2, 4, 12, 24
    e. Pitcher of beer (quarts): 1, 2, 4, 8
    f. Table height (inches): 10, 30, 50, 70
    g. Gallon of milk (pounds): 1, 2, 8, 16
    h. New York to Chicago (miles): 100, 400, 800, 1,600
    i. Can of soda (ounces): 4, 8, 12, 18

21. Which metric unit is most likely to be used in measuring the following?

    a. Width of a front door
    b. Volume of a large jug of wine
    c. Weight of a hamburger or hotdog
    d. Distance from a suburban house to the edge of the property line
    e. Distance from Hartford, Connecticut, to New Haven, Connecticut
    f. Weight of a bowling ball
    g. Height of a basketball player
    h. Your weight
    i. Diameter of a dime
    j. Length of the Mississippi River
    k. Weight of a dime

l. Width of camera film
m. Weight of ten grains of sand
n. Weight of a can of peach slices
o. Volume of a soda can

22. For each of the following items, identify the most likely approximate measurement from the choices given.

   a. Pencil length (cm): 0.5, 2, 20, 35, 70
   b. Volume of coffee cup (ml): 250, 500, 750, 1000, 1500
   c. Newborn baby's weight (kg): 1, 3.5, 8, 12, 20
   d. Automobile gasoline purchase (l): 1, 4, 20, 40, 120
   e. Volume of soda can (ml): 10, 35, 350, 700, 1500
   f. Length of a football field (m): 10, 50, 90, 130, 170
   g. Tablespoon of medicine (ml): 1, 5, 50, 500, 5000
   h. Temperature on a hot summer day (°C): 38°, 48°, 58°, 68°, 78°
   i. Temperature cool enough for a sweater (°C): 6°, 16°, 26°, 36°, 46°
   j. Outdoor iceskating temperature (°C): -8°, 8°, 18°, 28°, 38°

4. CALIBRATED SCALES

Every readable scale has markings on it. Some of the markings will be labeled and, very likely, some won't. To read the scale, you must understand what the markings represent. With this information, you can determine the reading on the gauge.

Problem: What is the reading on this gauge?

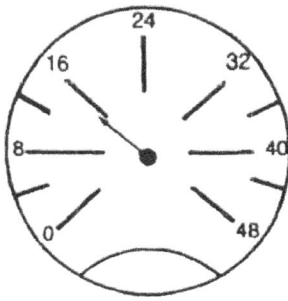

Solution: The longer scale markings represent multiples of 8, as labeled. The shorter markings are half-way between the longer ones. Thus, for example, the marking halfway between 8 and 16 represents 8 + 4 or 12. The pointer on the gauge lies between 12 and 16, but appears to be closer to 16 than to 12. The reading is approximately 15.

Problem: What reading is the arrow pointing to on this gauge?

8

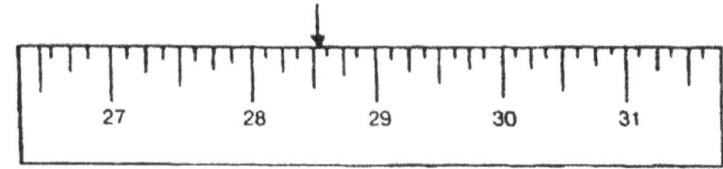

Solution: Here the long markings are marked off in increasing units of 1. Therefore, the next longest markings represent 1/2 units and the next longest 1/4 units; the shortest markings are half-way between 1/4 units and must represent 1/8 units. The arrow lies between 28 1/2 and 28 5/8. Since 1/2 = 4/8, the arrow lies half-way between the 1/8 unit markings. Half of 1/8 is 1/16. Thus, the reading is 28 1/2 + 1/16 = 28 8/16 + 1/16 = 28 9/16.

When reading gauges, be sure to figure out what the markings represent before you try to decipher the reading. Be careful, too. On some gauges the readings decrease as you move from left to right or from bottom to top.

EXERCISES

23. What is the approximate reading on this gauge?

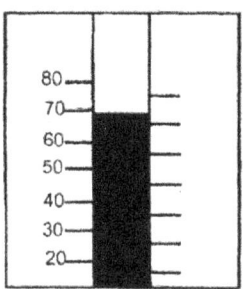

24. Estimate the reading on this gauge.

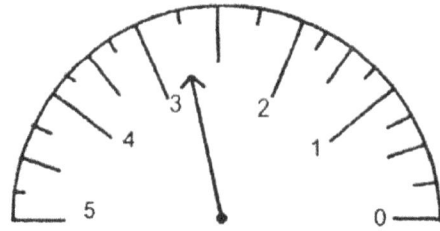

25. What is the reading on this gauge?

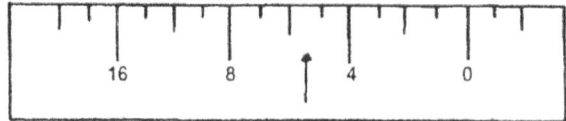

26. Read this scale.

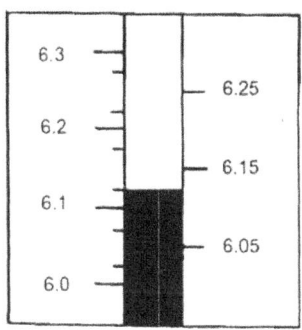

27. What measures are arrows a, b, c pointing to on this ruler?

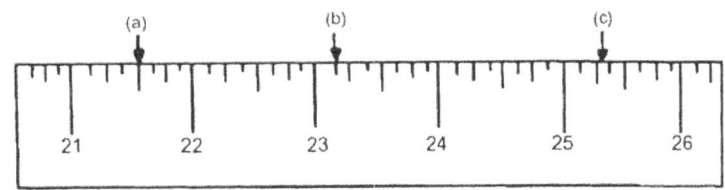

28. The pointer on this dial reads approximately

A. 28   B. 0.23   C. 0.27   D. 0.31

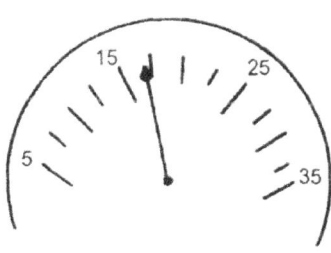

KEY (CORRECT ANSWERS)

1. 18 inches per year = 1 1/2 feet per year.

   1 1/2 x 25 = 25 + 12 1/2 = 37 1/2 feet in 25 years

2. 60,000 gal x 8 lbs/gal = 480,000 pounds of water
   480,000 lbs ÷ 2000 lbs/ton = 240 tons of water

3. $\dfrac{8 \text{ miles}}{12 \text{ minutes}} \times \dfrac{\overset{5}{6\cancel{0}} \text{ minutes}}{1 \text{ hour}} = \dfrac{40 \text{ miles}}{1 \text{ hour}} = 40$ miles per hour

   Alternatively: 12 minutes = 1/5 hour so she drove 8 miles in 1/5 hour. So, in one hour she would drive 40 miles or 40 miles per hour.

4. 56 yards = 168 feet. 168 feet x 40¢/foot = 6720¢
   56 yards cost $67.20

5. 10 lbs x 16 oz/lb = 160 oz 160 ÷ 6 = 25 2/3. You would need to buy 27 cans of cat food.

6. 81 ÷ 12 = 6 9/12 = 6 3/4 feet

7. One foot cost $15/4 = $3.75. Thus, 13 yards = 39 feet and cost $3.75 x 39 or $146.25.

8. The answer is 130. Each rope is 120 inches long. Since 120 ÷ 9 = 13 1/3, we can get 13 9-inch lengths from each rope. The extra 1/3 inch is unusable. We have 10 ropes so we can get 130 9-inch lengths altogether.

9. We need 43 half pints or 43/2 pints.

   $\dfrac{43}{2} \text{ pints} \cdot \dfrac{1 \text{ quart}}{2 \text{ pints}} \cdot \dfrac{1 \text{ gal}}{4 \text{ quarts}} = \dfrac{43}{16} \text{ gal}$

   = 2 11/16 gal. Since only whole gallons are available, we need 3 gallons.

10. 300 ml

11. 0.4 kg

12. 170 cm

13. 3100 cm per century. 31 m per century.

14. 1/2 kg = 500 grams. There are 100 5-gram units in 500 grams.
    Thus, you would pay .32 . 100 = $32.

15. 3m = 300 cm   300 ÷ 15 = 20 15-cm lengths

16. 7 bottles @ 1 liter each = 7 liters = 7000 ml
    7000 ÷ 750 = 9.3
    So, 10 bottles would be needed to exceed 7000 ml

17. 21.5 cm = 215 mm. Thus, the predicted recovery time is 215 days.

18. $\frac{\$42}{m} \cdot \frac{1000 m}{1 km}$ = $42000 per km. Thus, for 3.6 km, the cost is $42,000 x 3.6 = $151,200

19. (a) 250/4 = 125/2 = 62 1/2 doses per bottle.
    $3.20 v 125/2 = $3.20 x 2/125 = $6.40/125 or approximately
    $.05. Thus, each 4-ml dose costs about 5c. Since Paul takes 2 per day, his daily cost is about 10¢.

    (b) 4 l = 4000 ml. 4000 * 250 = 16 so there are 16 250-ml amounts in 4 l. Since each 250-ml amount cost $3.20, 4 l would cost $3.20 x 16 = $51.20

20. a. 14   d. 12   g. 8
    b. 3   e. 2   h. 800
    c. 1   f. 30   i. 12

21. a. m   f. kg   k. gm
    b. l   g. m   l. mm (e.g., 35 mm film)
    c. gm   h. kg   m. mg
    d. m   i. mm or cm   n. g
    e. km   j. km   o. ml

22. a. 20   e. 350   h. 38°
    b. 250   f. 90   i. 16°
    c. 3.5   g. 5   j. -8°
    d. 40

23. 68

24. 17

25. 5.5

26. 6.125

27. a. 21 1/2   b. 23 1/8   c. 25 5/16

28. c

TABLES OF USEFUL INFORMATION
Factors for Conversion of Units

Unit A measure	To convert to unit B multiply by:	To convert to unit A multiply by:	Unit B measure
ACCELERATION			
Foot/second^2	.3048	3.2808	Meter/second^2
Inch/second^2	2.540x10^{-2}	39.370	Meter/second^2
ANGLES			
Degree	.01745	57.296	Radian
Mils (circular)	.0562	17.78	Degrees, angular
Do	.008982	1.019	Radians
Do	5.067x10^{-10}	1.974x10^9	Meter^2
AREA			
Acre	4,047	2.471x10^{-4}	Meter^2
Do	4,840	.0002066	Square yards
Do	43,560	2.296x10^{-5}	Square feet
Do	.563x10^{-3}	640	Square miles
Circular Mil	5.067X10^{-10}	.1974	Meter^2
Foot^2	.09290	10.764	Meter^2
Inch^2	6.452	.155	Centimeters^2
Do	6.452x10^{-4}	1,550	Meter^2
Mile^2 (U.S. Statute)	2,589,988	3.861x10^{-7}	Meter^2
Do	2.59	.3861	Kilometers^2
Section	2,589,988	3.861x10^{-7}	Meter^2
Yard^2	.8361	1.1960	Meter^2

TABLES OF USEFUL INFORMATION
Factors for Conversion of Units

Unit A measure	To convert to unit B multiply by:	To convert to unit A multiply by:	Unit B measure
BENDING MOMENT (Torque)			
Dyne-centimetre	1.000×10^{-7}	1.000×10^{7}	Newton-meter
Kilogram-force-metre	9.8067	.102	Newton-meter
Ounce-force-inch	.007062	141.6	Newton-meter
Pound-force-inch	.11298	8.851	Newton-meter
Pound-force-foot	1.356	.7375	Newton-meter
(BENDING MOMENT OR TORQUE)/ LENGTH			
Pound-force-foot/inch	53.38	.01873	Newton-meter/meter
Pound-force-inch/inch	4.448	.2248	Newton-meter/meter
CAPACITY (See Volume) DENSITY (See Mass/Volume)			
ENERGY (Includes Work)			
Foot-pound	.001285	778.1	BTU
Do	.0003239	3088	Kilogram Calories
Do	3.766×10^{-7}	2655	Kilowatt-hours
Do	.1383	7.2330	Kilogram meters
Foot-pound-force	1.356	.7376	Joule
Kilowatt-hour	3 600,000	2.778×10^{-7}	Joule
Watt-hour	3,600	2.778×10^{-4}	Joule
Watt-second	1.000	1.000	Joule

TABLES OF USEFUL INFORMATION
Factors for Conversion of Units

Unit A measure	To convert to unit B multiply by:	To convert to unit A multiply by:	Unit B measure
FLOW (See Mass/ Time or Volume/Time)			
FORCE			
Dyne	1.000×10^{-5}	1.0×10^{5}	Newton
Kilogram-force....	9.807	.1020	Newton
Kip............	4448	.0002248	Newton
Pound-force (avoirdupois)	4.448	.2248	Newton
FORCE/AREA (See Pressure)			
FORCE/LENGTH			
Pound-force/inch..	175.1	.005710	Newton/Meter
Pound-force/foot ..	14.59	.06852	Newton/Meter
LENGTH			
Angstrom	1.000×10^{-10}	1.000×10^{10}	Meter
Fathom	1.829	.5468	Meter
Do.............	.0083	120	Cable lengths
Foot (U.S. Survey)..	.3048	3.281	Metre
Do.............	3.048×10^{-4}	3281.0	Kilometers
Do	.167	6	Fathoms
Do.............	.0606	16.5	Rods
Do.............	.0151	66	Chain
Do	.0015	660	Furlongs

TABLES OF USEFUL INFORMATION
Factors for Conversion of Units

Unit A measure	To convert to unit B multiply by:	To convert to unit A multiply by:	Unit B measure
Inch............	.02540	39.37	Meter
Do.............	2.54	.3937	Centimeters
League (Statute)..	4828.032	.0002071	Meter
Mil	2.540×10^{-5}	3937	Meter
Mile (U S Nautical)	1852.000	.00054	Meter
Do (U.S. Statute)..	1609	.0006214	Meter
Do	1.609	.6214	Kilometers
Do	.868	1,1515	Nautical Mile
Do	5,280	1.894×10^{-4}	Feet
Rod	5.029	.1988	Meter
Yard	.9144	1.094	Meter
LIGHT			
Foot candle......	10.76	.09290	Lumen/meter^2
Do	10.76	.09290	Lux
Lux............	1.000	1.000	Lumen/meter^2
MASS			
Grain	.0648	15.432	Grams
Gram...........	.001	1000	Kilogram
Kilogram-mass ...	1.000	1.000	Kilogram
Ounce-mass (avoirdupois)	.02835	35.26	Kilogram
Ounce..........	437.5	.002286	Grains

TABLES OF USEFUL INFORMATION
Factors for Conversion of Units

Unit A measure	To convert to unit B multiply by:	To convert to unit A multiply by:	Unit B measure
Pound-mass (avoirdupois)	.4536	2.205	Kilogram
Do	7000	.0001429	Grains
Pound	.0004464	2240	Long tons or gross tons
Slug	14.59	.06854	Kilogram
Ton (long, 2240 lbm)	1016.	.0009842	Kilogram
Do	1.016	0.9842	Tons (metric)
Ton (metric)	1000.00	0.001	Kilogram
Ton (short, 2000 lbm)	907.2	.001102	Kilogram
Do	.907	1.1023	Tons (metric)
Ton (Net or short-tons)	.8929	1.12	Ton (long or gross tons)
MASS/AREA			
Ounce-Mass/yard^2	.03391	29.49	Kilogram/meter^2
Pound-mass/foot^2	4.882	.2048	Kilogram/meter^2
MASS/CAPACITY (See Mass/Vol.)			
MASS/TIME (Includes Flow)			
Cubic feet per second (second feet)	60.0	.01667	Cubic feet per minute
Do	448.8	.002228	U.S. gallons per minute
Cubic feet per minute	7.481	.1337	Do.
Pound-mass/second	.4536	2.205	Kilogram/second
Pound-mass/minute	.007560	132.3	Kilogram/second

TABLES OF USEFUL INFORMATION
Factors for Conversion of Units

Unit A measure	To convert to unit B multiply by:	To convert to unit A multiply by:	Unit B measure
Ton (short, mass)/hour	.2520	3.968	Kilogram/second
MASS/VOLUME			
Gram/centimetre^3	1000.00	0.001	Kilogram/meter^3
Pound-mass/foot^3	16.02	.06243	Kilogram/meter^3
Do	.01602	62.43	Grams/centimeter^3 (specific gravity for solids)
Pound-mass/inch^3	27680	3.613×10^{-5}	Kilogram/meter^3
Slug/foot^3	515.4	.001940	Kilogram/meter^3
Ton (long, mass)/yard^3	1329	.0007525	Kilogram/meter^3
POWER			
Erg/second	1.000×10^{-7}	1.000×10^{7}	Watt
Foot-pound-force/hour	3.766×10^{-4}	2655	Watt
Horsepower	550	.001818	Foot-pounds per second
Horsepower (550 ft.lbf/s)	745.7	.001341	Watt
Horsepower (metric)	735.5	135.96	Watt
Do	75	.01333	Kilogram meters per second
Horsepower (water)	746.0	.001340	Watt
Horsepower (U.S.)	1.014	.9863	Horsepower (metric)
PRESSURE OR STRESS (Force/Area)			
Atmospheres (mean)	33.90	.02950	Feet of water

TABLES OF USEFUL INFORMATION
Factors for Conversion of Units

Unit A measure	To convert to unit B multiply by:	To convert to unit A multiply by:	Unit B measure
Atmospheres (mean)..	14.70	.0680	Pounds per square inch
Do............	29.92	.03342	Inches of mercury
Atmosphere (normal=769 torr.).	101325	9.869×10^{-6}	Pascal
Atmosphere (technical - 1 kgf/cm$^{2)}$.	98067	1.0197×10^{-5}	Pascal
Dyne/centimeter^2	.10000	10.00	Pascal
Feet of water	62.43	.01602	Pounds per square foot
Gram-force/centimeter^2	98.067	.010197	Pascal
Kilogram-force/centimeter^2	98067	1.097×10^{-5}	Pascal
Do............	14.22	.0703	Pounds per square inch
Kilogram-force/meter^2 ·	9.8067	.1020	Pascal
Do............	.2048	4.8824	Pounds per square foot
Kilogram-force/millimeter^2	9806650	1.10197×10^{-7}	Pascal
Kip/inch^2	6894757	1.450×10^{-7}	Pascal
Pound-force/foot^2	47.88	.02089	Pascal
Pound-force/inch^2 (psi) .	6894.757	.0001450	Pascal
Do............	2.036	.4912	Inches of mercury
SHIPPING			
Cubic feet	0.010	100.0	Register tons
Do	0.0250	40.0	U.S. shipping tons
Do.............	0.0238	42.0	British shipping tons

TABLES OF USEFUL INFORMATION Factors for Conversion of Units

Unit A measure	To convert to unit B multiply by:	To convert to unit A multiply by:	Unit B measure
SPEED (See Velocity)			
STRESS (See Pressure)			
TEMPERATURE			
Degree Celsius...	$t_k = t_c^o + 273.15$	$t_{c_o} = t_k - 273.15$	Kelvin
Degree Fahrenheit	$t_k = (t_{f_o} + 459.67)/1.8$	$t_{f_o} = 1.8(t_k) - 459.67$	Kelvin
Degree Rankine..	$t_{k_o} = t_R/1.8$	$t_{R_o} = 1.8 t_k$	Kelvin
Degree Fahrenheit	$t_c^o = (t_f^o - 32)/1.8$	$t_{f=1.8 t_c}^o + 32$	Degree Celsius
TORQUE (See Bending Moment).			
VELOCITY (Includes Speed)			
Foot/hour	8.467×10⁻⁵	11810	Meter/second
Foot/second.......	.3048	3.281	Meter/second
Inch/second.......	.02540	39.37	Meter/second
Kilometer/hour.....	.2778	3.600	Meter/second
Knot (International).	.5144	1.944	Meter/second
Miles/hoar	1.467	.6818	Feet/second
Miles/hour	.4470	2.237	Meter/second
Do	1.609	.6214	Kilometers/hour
Do	.8684	1.1516	Knots
Mile/minute	26.82	.03728	Meter/second
Mile/second.......	1609	.0006214	Do.

TABLES OF USEFUL INFORMATION
Factors for Conversion of Units

Unit A measure	To convert to unit B multiply by:	To convert to unit A multiply by:	Unit B measure
VOLUME			
Acre-foot	1233.5	.00081071	Meter^3
Barrel (petroleum, 42 gal.)	.1590	6.290	Do.
Board foot	.002360	423.8	Do.
Bushel (U.S.)	.03524	28.38	Do.
Cup	.0002366	4,227	Do.
Fluid ounce (U.S.)	2.9574x10^{-5}	33,814	Do.
Foot^3	.02832	35.31	Do.
Do	1728	0.000579	Inches^3
Do	7.481	.1337	Gallons (U.S.)
Do	6.229	.1605	Gallons (Imperial) Bushels (U.S.)
Do	.8036	1.2445	
Do	12	.0833	Board feet
Do	.007813	128	Cords of wood
Do	28.317	.03531	Liters
Gallon (Canadian liquid)	.0045461	219.97	Meter^3
Gallon (U.S. liquid)	.003785	264.2	Do.
Do	.8325	1.201	Gallons (Imperial)
Do	.03175	31.5	Barrels Liter
Do	3.785	.2672	Meter^3
Gallon (U.S. dry)	.0044049	227.02	

TABLES OF USEFUL INFORMATION
Factors for Conversion of Units

Unit A measure	To convert to unit B multiply by:	To convert to unit A multiply by:	Unit B measure
Inch^3	1.6387x10^{-5}	61,024	Meter^3
Do	16.38716	.061	Centimeters^3
Do	.5541	1.805	Fluid ounces (U.S.)
Litre	.0010	1000	Meter^3
Ounce (U.S. fluid)	2.957353x10^{-5}	33,814	Do.
Pint (U.S. dry)	5.506x10^{-4}	1,816.2	Do.
Pint (U.S. liquid)	4.7318x10^{-4}	2,113.4	Do.
Pounds/yard^3	.0593	16.856	Kilograms/hectoliter
Quart (U.S. dry)	1.101221x10^{-3}	908.1	Meter^3
Quart (U.S. liquid)	9.464x10^{-4}	1057	Do.
Do	.946	1.0569	Liters
Ton (register)	2.832	.3532	Meter^3
Yard^3	.76456	1.308	Meter^3
VOLUME/TIME (Includes Flow)			
Foot^3/minute	4.719x10^{-4}	2,118.9	Meter^3/second
Foot^3/second	2.831x10^{-2}	35.31	Do.
Inch^3/minute	2.7312x10^{-7}	3,661,400	Do.
Yard^3/minute	.01274	78.48	Do.
Gallon (U.S. liquid)/day	4.3813x10^{-8}	22,824,000	Do.
Gallon (U.S. liquid)/minute	6.309x10^{-5}	15,850	Do.

TABLES OF USEFUL INFORMATION
Factors for Conversion of Units

Unit A measure	To convert to unit B multiply by:	To convert to unit A multiply by:	Unit B measure
WEIGHT, LINEAR			
Pounds/foot	1.488	.672	Kilograms per meter
Pounds/yard	.496	2.016	Do.
WORK (See Energy)			

Made in United States
North Haven, CT
17 August 2022